Research Series on the Chinese Dream and China's Development Path

Drawing on a large body of empirical studies done over the last two decades, the *Research Series on the Chinese Dream and China's Development Path* seeks to provide its readers with in-depth analyses of the past and present, and forecasts for the future course of China's development. Thanks to the adoption of Socialism with Chinese characteristics, and the implementation of comprehensive reform and opening, China has made tremendous achievements in areas such as political reform, economic development, and social construction, and is making great strides towards the realization of the Chinese dream of national rejuvenation. In addition to presenting a detailed account of many of these achievements, the authors also discuss what lessons other countries can learn from China's experience. This series will be an invaluable companion to every researcher who is trying to gain a deeper understanding of the development model, path and experience unique to China.

More information about this series at http://www.springer.com/series/13571

Zengyi Xie

Labor Law in China

Progress and Challenges

SSAP

Springer

Zengyi Xie
Institute of Law
Chinese Academy of Social Sciences
Beijing, China

Sponsored by Innovation Project of CASS

ISSN 2363-6866 ISSN 2363-6874 (electronic)
Research Series on the Chinese Dream and China's Development Path
ISBN 978-3-662-46928-6 ISBN 978-3-662-46929-3 (eBook)
DOI 10.1007/978-3-662-46929-3

Library of Congress Control Number: 2015938302

Springer Heidelberg New York Dordrecht London

Printed on acid-free paper

Springer-Verlag GmbH Berlin Heidelberg is part of Springer Science+Business Media (www.springer.com)

Acknowledgments

After a relatively short gestation period, the *Research Series on the Chinese Dream and China's Development Path* has started to bear fruit. We have, first and foremost, the books' authors and editors to thank for making this possible. And it was the hard work by many people at Social Sciences Academic Press and Springer, the two collaborating publishers, that made it a reality. We are deeply grateful to all of them.

Mr. Xie Shouguang, president of Social Sciences Academic Press (SSAP), is the mastermind behind the project. In addition to defining the key missions to be accomplished by it and setting down the basic parameters for the project's execution, as the work has unfolded, Mr. Xie has provided critical input pertaining to its every aspect and at every step of the way. Thanks to the deft coordination by Ms. Li Yanling, all the constantly moving parts of the project, especially those on the SSAP side, are securely held together and as well synchronized as is feasible for a project of this scale. Ms. Gao Jing, unfailingly diligent and meticulous, makes sure every aspect of each Chinese manuscript meets the highest standards for both publishers, something of critical importance to all subsequent steps in the publishing process. That high-quality, if also at times stylistically as well as technically challenging, scholarly writing in Chinese has turned into decent, readable English that readers see on these pages is largely thanks to Ms. Liang Fan, who oversees translator recruitment and translation quality control.

Ten other members of the SSAP staff have been intimately involved, primarily in the capacity of in-house editors, in the preparation of the Chinese manuscripts. It is time-consuming work that requires attention to details, and each of them has done this and is continuing to do this with superb skills. They are, in alphabetical order, Mr. Cai Jihui, Ms. Liu Xiaojun, Mr. Ren Wenwu, Ms. Shi Xiaolin, Ms. Song Yuehua, Mr. Tong Genxing, Ms. Wu Dan, Ms. Yao Dongmei, Ms. Yun Wei, and Ms. Zhou Qiong. In addition, Xie Shouguang and Li Yanling have also taken part in this work.

Ms. Liu Xiaojun is the SSAP in-house editor for the current volume.

Our appreciation is also owed to Ms. Li Yan, Mr. Chai Ning, Ms. Wang Lei, and Ms. Xu Yi from Springer Beijing Representative Office. Their strong support for the

SSAP team in various aspects of the project helped to make the latter's work that much easier than it would have otherwise been.

We thank Ms. Sonia Jia Song for translating this book and Mr. Daniel J. Knudsen for his work as the polisher. Besides, we thank the author, Mr. Zengyi Xie, for his great contribution to the English manuscript.

Last, but certainly not least, it must be mentioned that funding for this project comes from the Ministry of Finance of the People's Republic of China. Our profound gratitude, if we can be forgiven for a bit of apophasis, goes without saying.

Social Sciences Academic Press
Springer

About the Book

China is the most populous country with the largest labor force, and its approach to labor protection has drawn wide attention at home and abroad. As globalization and international mobility of capital and labor increase, even more attention is focused on labor protection.

In *Labor Law in China: Progress and Challenges*, the author explains the development of the concept and system of labor protection in China in the era of reform and opening up and describes the progress and challenges of labor law legislation and enforcement. This book is the first treatise on China's labor law by a Chinese scholar published in English outside China. It combines theory and practice from both Chinese and international perspectives.

The book covers a wide range of Chinese labor laws, with a focus on those concerning individual workers. Topics covered include the definition of the employer and the employee and their basic rights and obligations; legislation on employment nondiscrimination, especially nondiscrimination concerning the disabled in employment and the quota mechanism for employment of the disabled; laws and regulations regarding labor dispatch; minimum wage system; termination of labor contracts; work-related injury compensation system; labor inspection system and employers' liabilities; and labor dispute resolution. While elaborating on current labor laws in China, the book also introduces the underlying rationale for, and real-world application of, these laws. *Labor Law in China: Progress and Challenges* also points out the challenges of labor law legislation itself as well as its application and enforcement. The book also offers suggestions for improving the labor law system. In the author's view, great progress has been made in Chinese labor law. Yet, better legislation is required; application and enforcement need to be strengthened, and China could benefit from drawing upon the experiences of other countries.

While primarily based on Chinese labor law and its enforcement, the author adopts a comparative approach, which will help those in human resource management in Chinese companies and Chinese and foreign academics, to gain a better understanding of the current state of labor laws in China. Suggestions for improvement can also serve as useful references for the Chinese legislature and China's labor law enforcement agencies.

Labor Law in China: Progress and Challenges opens a window to understand labor laws in China and helps improve China's labor rights protection.

About the Author

Zengyi Xie Ph.D. in law, is Associate Professor at the Institute of Law, Chinese Academy of Social Sciences (CASS). He is also a member of the Academic Committee and Deputy Secretary-General of China's Labor and Social Law Association. He has previously been a visiting scholar at the University of Oxford, Columbia University, and Harvard University. Professor Xie specializes in labor law and social security law. He has published three books: *Labor Law in China: Reform and Improvements* (2015), *Rethinking China's Labor Law* (2011) and *Conflict of Interests in Demutualized Stock Exchanges* (2007). His many articles have appeared in different Chinese and foreign legal journals, including *CASS Journal* of *Law* and *China Law Review.* Professor Xie serves as legal counsel for the All-China Federation of Trade Unions. In 2014, the China Law Society nominated Professor Xie for the seventh Ten Most Outstanding Young Chinese Legal Scholars Award.

Contents

Introduction

Since the era of reform and opening up began, China's labor force has confronted a market economy and experienced gradual change along with a deepening of the reforms of the economic system and enterprise management. Labor relationships between employers and employees are now established through labor contracts that give both the employer and employee the decision-making power to hire or to be hired. The market is playing an increasingly important role in the establishment and operation of a labor relationship. Yet, the imbalance of status and power between the individual worker and the employer makes workers vulnerable to violations of their rights and interests. Therefore, the law must provide special protection to workers so as to safeguard their basic rights and dignity.

China's labor law legislation has made remarkable progress since China embarked on the path to a market economy. Following the Labor Law's enactment in 1994, China's legislature has adopted more labor laws and regulations, such as Labor Contract Law, Employment Promotion Law, Labor Dispute Mediation and Arbitration Law, Workplace Safety Law, and Social Insurance Law. An overall labor law framework is now in place. But on the whole, many provisions tend to be too general to be enforceable. In fact, labor law legislation only lays the foundation for labor protection. Implementation and enforcement are more important. Currently, major enforcement mechanisms entail labor inspection, labor mediation, arbitration, and litigation. Although enforcement of labor laws has been strengthened, these mechanisms are facing many difficulties and challenges and need to be further improved.

China is the world's most populous country with the largest labor force. Its labor relations are extremely complex. The main challenges China is facing include how to balance the daunting task of economic development against labor protection, how to deal with the increasing international mobility of capital and labor under globalization, and how to handle the huge impact of an aging population on the labor market and labor protection. In particular, as the largest developing country, China is still going through the process of urbanization and industrialization. A certain degree of "duality" exists in the labor market because of the gap between the labor force from urban and rural areas. In 2013, migrant workers totaled 268.94 million in China; their presence makes labor protection even harder.

Topics covered in this book include the definition of the employer and the employee and their basic rights and duties; legislation on employment antidiscrimination, especially antidiscrimination against the disabled and the quota system for the disabled; regulation on labor dispatch; minimum wage system, working hours, and holidays; termination of labor contracts; work-related injury compensation system; labor inspection system and employers' liabilities; and labor dispute resolution. This book analyzes progress made and challenges remaining in these areas. It also makes reference to the theories and practices in other countries with the goal of learning what could be beneficial to China.

Chapter 1
The Meaning of a Labor Relationship and Identification of the Employee and the Employer

Labor law primarily regulates labor relationships.[1] Yet neither the *Labor Law* nor the *Labor Contract Law* contain clear provisions about what a labor relationship entails. This lack of clarity has caused difficulties in fixing labor relationships and applying labor laws in practice. Therefore, the connotation of labor relationship and criteria of identification has become an important issue in the theory and practice of labor law.

1.1 The Meaning of a Labor Relationship

The concept of a "labor relationship" developed from the traditional "employment relationship", a concept previously covered in civil law or private law. During the early industrial period, private law governed the employment relationship. The civil codes of major continental law countries reflected this model. For example, Article 611 to 630 of the *German Civil Codes* contains provisions on an "employment contract."[2] An employment relationship gave emphasis to labor service as the subject of a contract and assumed equal status of the parties. Later, the disparity of status between the parties in an employment relationship and social factors that came into play were recognized. An employment relationship would involve public interest or personal rights issues, which might not be decided entirely by the will of parties. Thus, legislators gradually realized and accepted the concept of a labor contract, and "employment contract" was gradually replaced by "labor contract" in some countries.

Labor policies and legislation witnessed great changes during the "labor contract" era: the states adopted labor protection laws and regulations to impose duties on the employer in the sense of public interest law to offer protection for the workers;

---

[1] Huai Guan, Jia Lin (ed.), *Labor Law*, China Renmin University Press, 2006, p. 5.

[2] Weizuo Chen, trans. *German Civil Codes,* Law Press, 2006, p. 231.

Z. Xie, *Labor Law in China*, Research Series on the Chinese Dream and China's Development Path, DOI 10.1007/978-3-662-46929-3_1

social factors began to be considered, and labor contract laws of important social significance were enacted; a mechanism of collective bargaining was used to turn conflict between the employer and employee to collaboration; social insurance policies were adopted; and labor law tribunals were established, and so on.[3] For instance, although the concept of the employment contract remained in the *German Civil Codes*, numerous special labor protection laws were enacted in addition to the *Civil Codes*, such as the Law on Dismissal Protection. Therefore, the labor contract was governed by labor laws outside of civil codes, which emphasized the subordinate position of the employee to the employer, and recognized that because the parties were not entirely equal in power special protection was needed for the employee.

Legislation and case law of most countries indicate that the main feature of labor contract relationship lies in the special subordinate position of the employee in the contract. For example, the German scholars write that "an employee is a person who is obligated to work for somebody else on the basis of a private contract in a relationship of personal subordination".[4] The Employment Appeal Tribunal in United Kingdom has also held: "The reason why employees need the protection of labor law is because they are in a subordinate and dependent position in relation to the employer."[5]

The determination of a labor relationship under labor laws is complex. In many countries, the concepts of "employer" and "employee" are defined by the relevant legislation and case law. Special emphasis is placed on "subordination" as an essential criterion for determining whether a labor relationship exists and whether the labor law is applicable.

1.2 Basic Criteria for Identifying a Labor Relationship

Article 2 of the *Labor Contract Law* stipulates that "[t]his law is applicable to the formation, performance, modification, rescission, and termination of a labor contract established between a worker and an enterprise, individually-owned business, or a private non-enterprise organization within the People's Republic of China." The law provides a clear coverage of an employer but does not state what constitutes a "labor relationship" and its determining criteria, and the law is unclear about the definition of an employee.

In 2005, the Ministry of Labor and Social Security (Now the Ministry of Human Resources and Social Security) issued the *Notice of Certain Issues on Establishing a Labor Relationship*, which provided a basic method for determining a labor relationship. It stated: "a labor relationship is deemed established even when there is no

[3] Yueqin Huang, *New Commentaries on the Labor Law*, China University of Political Science and Law Press, 2003.

[4] Manfred Weiss and Marlene Schmidt, *Labor Law and Industrial Relations in Germany*, Kluwer Law International, 2008, p. 45.

[5] A. C. L. Davies, *Perspectives on Labor Law*, Cambridge University Press, 2004, p. 88.

written labor contract if the following conditions exist: (1) the employer and employee meet the legal qualification prescribed by laws and regulations; (2) various workplace rules made by the employer in accordance with the law are applicable to the employee, and the employee is under control of the employer and performs paid labor assigned by the employer; (3) labor provided by the employee is a part of the business of the employer."[6] According to this rule, an employee and a labor relationship can only exist under the condition that "the employee" is under the control and management of the employer and the work of "the employee" is part of the employer's business. In practice, these are the criteria used by arbitration agencies and courts when determining whether a labor relationship existed. However, the determination of a labor relationship can be complex. Therefore, in making such determinations, primary consideration should be given to whether "the employer" exerts substantial control on "the employee". At the same time, other factors should be taken into account, including whether "the employee" joins the "employer" and becomes its member and who takes the risk of the losses of the business, and so on.

1.3 Special Categories of Employees

1.3.1 Domestic Workers

There are a huge number of domestic workers in China. But because many of them are directly employed by families, and many times without registration, it is difficult to determine an exact figure. However, statistics show that there were 15 million domestic workers in China in 2010.[7] Protection of domestic workers' rights has been gaining attention in recent years. On June 16, 2011, the General Conference of the International Labor Organization (ILO) adopted the *Convention Concerning Decent Work for Domestic Workers* (hereinafter the "*Convention*").[8] The *Convention* recognized "the significant contribution of domestic workers to the global economy, which includes increasing paid job opportunities for female and male workers with family responsibilities, greater scope for caring for aging populations, children, and persons with a disability, and substantial income transfers within and between countries."[9] The *Convention* also pointed out that domestic work continues to be undervalued and invisible, and many female domestic workers are particularly vulnerable to discrimination in respect of conditions of employment and of work and other abuses of human rights. The *Convention* further noted in developing countries

[6] Ministry of Labor and Social Security, *Notice of Certain Issues on Establishing a Labor Relationship* (2005, No.12), Article 1.

[7] Dan Ma, *Current Situation and Issues Regarding Domestic Workers in Beijing,* Rule of Law and Society, No.1, 2011, pp. 175–176.

[8] On June 16, 2011, the General Conference of the International Labor Organization adopted the *Convention Concerning Decent Work for Domestic Workers*.

[9] Preamble, *Convention Concerning Decent Work for Domestic Workers*, 2011.

with historically scarce opportunities for formal employment, domestic workers remain among the most marginalized.[10] Thus, many countries face the task of how to provide protection for domestic workers. Countries have adopted different approaches in this regard, which in general fall into three categories: (1) making labor laws and regulations fully applicable, (2) making them partially applicable, and (3) making them inapplicable to domestic workers.[11]

1.3.1.1 Special Characteristics of Domestic Workers

Currently China does not have laws or administrative regulations explicitly addressing domestic workers. Article 2 of the *Explanation of Certain Provisions of Labor Law* issued by the Ministry of Labor (Now the Ministry of Human Resources and Social Security) in 1994 delineated that the *Labor Law* was not applicable to domestic workers. A judicial interpretation of China's Supreme Court also expressly stipulated that "disputes between a family or an individual and a domestic worker" are not considered labor disputes.[12] That is, a domestic worker employed by a family or an individual does not qualify as an "employee" and is thus not protected by the labor law. The position of the Supreme Court's judicial interpretation could be justified since, compared to regular employees, domestic workers are different and special in the following aspects:

First, domestic workers are employed in special workplace. Domestic workers mainly work in a private home. Under the Convention's definition, "the term *domestic work* means work performed in or for a household or households." Since households are "private" property and usually not open to the public, the domestic worker is in a "private" space. Some domestic workers even live in the home of the employer and are hardly seen by the outside world. This makes the employee vulnerable in terms of personal safety and privacy, and protection by law is necessary in this respect. Also domestic workers are scattered in different households and face difficulties in organizing into trade unions to conduct collective bargaining and take collective actions, which restricts the collective rights of this group as a whole.

Second, domestic workers have special job duties. Although domestic workers provide labor services, those services are related to domestic chores such as cleaning, driving, cooking, taking care of children or the elderly. Job duties are not clear-cut and are not easy to quantify in advance, and the outcome of services is not easy to measure. Also, domestic worker's work time is flexible, hard to define, and distinguishing between work time and rest time for domestic workers proves difficult. Moreover, usually only one domestic worker is employed by the same

[10] Preamble, *Convention Concerning Decent Work for Domestic Workers*, 2011.

[11] Zengyi Xie, *Beyond the Rules of the Employment and Labor Contract – Legal Concept and Mechanism for Protection of Domestic Workers,* Tsinghua Law Review, No. 6, 2012, p. 77.

[12] *The Interpretation of Applicable Laws in Adjudicating Labor Disputes of the Supreme Peoples' Court* (II), 2006, Article 7.

employer. Thus, apart from supervision of the employer, there is little cooperation and supervision among domestic workers.

Third, domestic workers face special gender issues. Although "domestic worker" is a neutral term, in reality, compared to regular workers, domestic workers' education and level of professionalism is relatively low and the ability to safeguard their rights relatively weak. As far as gender is concerned, female domestic workers are far more prevalent than male. One statistic shows that currently, over 96 % domestic workers in China are female workers.[13] Therefore, protection of domestic workers is not only an issue of employment contract and labor protection but also one of gender equality.

Fourth, domestic workers have special mobility. Due to special nature of their work and factors such as personal trust between the employee and employer, domestic workers are more mobile than other workers. Especially in China, many domestic workers are not professionals. They are often from other parts of the country rather than the city they are working, and once they have a choice between staying home to farm, taking care of their own family, or engaging in other activities, they will leave the city for home. For instance, the result of a survey project group in Tianjin City conducted in November 2010 indicated that 97 % of domestic workers stayed with the employer for less than a year.[14] This fully demonstrates domestic workers' mobility.

In addition, many domestic workers who are immigrants from other countries or regions, which makes them vulnerable, due to their less education, low skills, and nationality.

Two legal issues flow from the above facts. First, because of the special features of the work place – being private, lacking public access, being scattered, and with the workers themselves being in a disadvantaged position – domestic workers are vulnerable to violation of their rights. The law needs to provide special protection for them. From this point of view, the regular employment contract rules do not meet the need for protection of domestic workers. Therefore, special protective regulations should be enacted in addition to the protections in their employment contracts.

Second, the "employer" of domestic workers is also different from regular employers. The employer of a domestic worker is a family or individual, not a for-profit organization. Given this, the flexibility of the domestic work, and other factors, such as the trust and relationships between the employer and the employee, it would be unnecessary as well as unrealistic to impose too many legal duties over the employer.

---

[13] Wei Zhang, *Analysis of Social and Legal Protection for Domestic Workers from the Perspective of Gender Mainstreaming,* Hebei Law Review, 2010, No.8, p. 99.

[14] The survey project group distributed 400 Questionnaires. See Minghui Liu, *Obstacles and Approaches for Domestic Workers to Gain the Right to Labor and Social Security Protection,* Journal of the Southwest Nationality University (Liberal Arts and Social Science), 2011, No.5, p. 121.

Therefore, it would be inappropriate to include domestic workers in the regulatory scope of the labor law. Of course, not fully including domestic workers in the protective scope of the *Labor Law* does not mean they should not be offered any legal protection. In light of the above features of domestic workers, part of labor law rules or special rules outside labor law should be provided to protect domestic workers.

1.3.1.2 How to Provide Legal Protection for Domestic Workers

Under the current legal framework, a feasible approach would be to fully consider the special nature of domestic workers and adopt separate protective regulations for domestic workers. For aspects not covered by the regulations, the relevant provisions of civil law rules could govern. Based on the special characteristics of domestic workers, the *Convention*, and current Chinese labor laws, future protective regulations for domestic workers should cover the following:

First, basic personal rights.

Since domestic workers and the employers have a close personal contractual relationship and the workplace is usually in the household of the employer, closed and private, the personal rights of the domestic worker should be protected when they are providing domestic service. Article 3 of the *Convention* states: "Each Member shall take measures to ensure the effective promotion and protection of the human rights of all domestic workers, as set out in this *Convention*," and "[e]ach Member shall, in relation to domestic workers, take the measures set out in this *Convention* to respect, promote and realize the fundamental principles and rights at work." Legislation concerning domestic workers in China should specifically stipulate that domestic workers enjoy personal freedom and are free from forced labor, abuse, violence, and harassment, and child labor is forbidden. Since domestic workers provide services or live in the household of the employer, their right to privacy must be protected as well. And domestic workers should not be discriminated against in employment and occupation.[15]

Second, decent work environment and work conditions.

Domestic workers are engaged in domestic chores in a closed workplace with special job duties. Therefore the employer should provide a safe and healthy work environment. The *Convention* clearly states that each Member shall take measures to ensure that domestic workers, like workers generally, enjoy fair terms of employment as well as decent working conditions. Every domestic worker has the right to a safe and healthy working environment. The *Guiding Opinions on Developing Household Service by the State Council General Office*[16] also instructs that "relevant agencies of the State Council will research to develop labor and employment policies and labor standards that are suitable to the characteristics of domestic ser-

[15] See *Convention Concerning Decent Work for Domestic Workers*, 2011, Articles 3, 5, 6.

[16] See *Guiding Opinion on Developing Domestic Service* issued by the General Office of the State Council, 2010.

vice and to promote decent work for domestic workers." Accordingly, decent work is a goal in China, therefore providing a decent work environment and conditions by the employer should be a general obligation clause in the future legislation for domestic workers.

Third, minimum labor and social security standards.

Labor standards concerning services provided by domestic workers include work hours, rest and holiday, wage, and social security. Although it's difficult to apply all general labor law provisions to domestic workers, the nature of their labor service makes it compulsory to set minimum labor and social security standards to protect their basic rights as providers of labor.

Since obtaining remuneration is the basic purpose of providing labor service, minimum wage standards should apply. Also, since domestic workers' work hours are flexible, the minimum wage applied should be a minimum *hourly* wage. And sometimes it is difficult to distinguish between domestic workers' work time and rest time because of the flexibility of their work. It is hard to apply general labor law work hour rules to domestic workers. Therefore, maximum work hours in the legislation could be relatively longer. For instance, legislation could provide that their daily work hours cannot exceed 10 h. However, in order to protect domestic workers' rights of health and rest, rules concerning rest should be provided. For full- time domestic workers, the legislation could prescribe that weekly rest provided by the employer must be for at least 24 consecutive hours.[17]

Social security standards are also an important issue for protection of domestic workers. The *Convention* stresses that "each Member shall take appropriate measures, in accordance with national laws and regulations and with due regard for the specific characteristics of domestic work, to ensure that domestic workers enjoy conditions that are not less favorable than those applicable to workers generally in respect of social security protection, including with respect to maternity." At the same time, the *Convention* cautions that the measures referred to may be applied progressively.[18] According to the current Chinese *Social Insurance Law,* domestic workers can join pension insurance and medical insurance plans as "other workers with flexible employment,"[19] but they cannot join unemployment insurance, work-related injury insurance, and maternity insurance plans. In order to support the development of domestic service and to protect the rights of domestic workers, like regular "workers," domestic workers should be covered by all the five categories of social insurance.

Four, contract law rights and dismissal protection.

---

[17]Article 10 of the *Convention Concerning Decent Work for Domestic Workers* states: Each Member shall take measures towards ensuring equal treatment between domestic workers and workers generally in relation to normal hours of work, overtime compensation, periods of daily and weekly rest and paid annual leave, taking into account the special characteristics of domestic work. And also weekly rest shall be at least 24 consecutive hours.

[18]Article 14 of the *Convention Concerning Decent Work for Domestic Workers.*

[19]Article 10 and 23 of the *Social Insurance Law.*

Since the essence of the relationship between the domestic worker and employer is a contractual relationship, domestic workers should be able to enjoy the rights provided by contract law. Apart from general rights provided by contract law, Article 7 of the *Convention* also provides domestic workers the right to know, i.e., domestic workers are informed of their terms and conditions of employment in an appropriate, verifiable, and easily understandable manner. By the same token, relevant legislation in China should prescribe domestic workers' right to be informed of the terms and conditions of the contract. In addition, the termination provision in a domestic worker's contract is an important legal issue. Since termination of a labor contract and protection from dismissal is a core issue in labor law, it is of particular importance whether the dismissal protection rules in labor law apply to domestic workers. Considering that dismissal protection rules in labor law are primarily designed for organized enterprises with a certain number of employees and job positions, and such employers have relatively strong organizational and management abilities, it is difficult to apply similar dismissal protection rules to the employer of the domestic worker who is either a family or an individual. In other words, dismissal protection provisions in the labor law should not be applicable to domestic workers.

The *Convention* also shows some flexibility in contract termination for domestic workers and does not require the same protection accorded to employees under the labor law. Article 7 of the *Convention* only imposes a notice obligation on the employer in a situation of dismissal, i.e., terms and conditions relating to the termination of employment can be included in the contract, including any period of notice required for dismissal by either the domestic worker or the employer. The *Convention* does not specify the legal cause of dismissal, or other procedure requirement of dismissal.

Five, the right to administrative and judicial remedies.

The social nature of domestic workers renders administrative monitoring necessary. However, a family or an individual employer is quite different from an organized and open enterprise, and such an employer should not be overburdened. Also, consideration should be given as to whether involvement of administrative agencies will affect protection of family privacy and whether administrative agencies have the resources for such monitoring. Therefore, administrative monitoring of domestic workers should only focus on matters concerning their basic rights, such as personal safety, a safe and healthy work environment, and the minimum wage, and so on. For general contract disputes, the parties should seek remedies from courts.

In short, relevant legislation in China should be based on general labor contract law while taking into consideration the special characteristics of domestic workers and content of the *Convention*; it should make adjustments of certain labor law provisions so they become applicable to domestic workers and provide protections for their basic rights, including a safe work environment and job conditions, work hours, rest and holiday, minimum wage, and social insurance.[20]

---

[20] Zengyi Xie, *Beyond the Rules of the Employment and Labor Contract – Legal Concept and Mechanism for Protection of Domestic Workers,* Tsinghua Law Review, 2012, No. 6, p. 79.

1.3.2 *Post-Retirement Age Individuals Who Return or Remain in the Workforce*

It has been a hotly debated academic and practical issue whether post-retirement age workers are "employees" and whether they should be protected under the labor law in China. The *Labor Contract Law* stipulates that a labor contract ends when an employee begins to enjoy basic pension benefits prescribed by law.[21] According to this provision, if the post-retirement age worker does not enjoy basic pension benefits, then a labor contract relationship exists and labor laws apply. If the post-retirement age worker begins to enjoy the pension insurance benefits, however, then the labor contract terminates and the post-retirement age worker is not protected by the labor law. The *Regulations for the Implementation of Labor Contract Law* (2008) further specify that the labor contract terminates when the employee reaches legal retirement age.[22] This provision differs from the provision of the *Labor Contract Law* in that, according to this provision, as long as the employee reaches the legal retirement age, the labor contract automatically ends and this person is no longer under the protection of the labor law regardless of whether this person is enjoying pension benefits.

In legal practice, according to the Supreme People's Court's judicial interpretation, when there is a labor dispute between an employer and the post-retirement age worker who is already enjoying pension or retirement benefits, and a lawsuit is filed with a court, the court should not adjudicate it as it would a labor relationship case.[23] This shows the Supreme People's Court consistency with the *Labor Contract Law* on this issue.

In general, the *Labor Contract Law* and rules about its implementation do not recognize the employee status of post-retirement age workers and the labor law does not protect them. This rule maybe problematic, as it lacks theoretical basis, and is not conducive to labor protection for this group of workers; it is also a misreading of the legal meaning of "retirement." The reasons are as follows.

1.3.2.1 The Right to Work Is a Constitutional Right Which Should Be Enjoyed by All

From a theoretical perspective, the right to work is a constitutional right that should be enjoyed by all regardless of age. It is also regarded as a basic human right. International human right conventions and related documents treat the right to work as an important human right that should not be easily denied. Article 23 of the *Universal Declaration of Human Rights* states that everyone has the right to work,

---

[21] The *Labor Contract Law*, Article 44.

[22] *Implementation Regulations of the Labor Contract Law*, 2008, Article 21.

[23] *The Interpretation of Applicable Laws in Adjudicating Labor Disputes of the Supreme People's Court* (III), 2010, Article 7.

to free choice of employment, to just and favorable conditions of work, and to protection against unemployment. This Declaration does not impose an age limit on this right. Article 6 of the *International Covenant on Economic, Social and Cultural Rights* also states: "The States Parties to the present Covenant recognize the right to work, which includes the right of everyone to the opportunity to gain his living by work which he freely chooses or accepts, and will take appropriate steps to safeguard this right." Therefore, unless there is sufficient reason, the state cannot arbitrarily deprive citizens of basic rights like the right to work. Apart from the prohibition on child labor, the *International Covenant on Economic, Social and Cultural Rights* also does not specify that the right to work is not applicable to people over a certain age. In other words, except for children, everyone should enjoy the right to work without limitation of age.

Article 34 of the Chinese Constitution states: "citizens of the People's Republic of China have the right and duty to work," which does not state an age limit. Article 15 of the *Labor Law* provides: "the employer is prohibited from hiring minors under the age of 16." This law only prohibits an employer from hiring child labor but does not prohibit an employer from hiring a person who has reached the retirement age. Therefore, excluding people who have reached legal retirement age from labor law protection does not have a strong legal basis in the Constitution or *Labor Law*.

1.3.2.2 The Employment Relationship of Post-Retirement Age Workers Conforms with the Characteristic of a Labor Relationship

The current *Labor Law* is applicable to all enterprises, individually-owned businesses, and employees who have formed a labor relationship with the above-mentioned entities within the People's Republic of China.[24] Thus, so long as the parties have a labor relationship, the *Labor Law* is applicable. And the criteria for a labor relationship are an objective standard that has no direct relation to age.

According to the theory and practice, the subordination relationship of the employee to the employer is the basic criterion for determining whether a labor relationship exists. As long as this subordination relationship exists, a labor relationship is established, regardless of age. Whether an employee has reached retirement age does not affect the existence of the subordination relationship.

Also, if an employee has worked for an employer for a long time, and the employee continues to work on the same job for the employer after reaching retirement age, then the labor relationship has not changed. If the rigid rule of automatic termination of a labor contract once the employee reaches retirement age is followed, then the employee would have a totally different legal relationship with the employer before and after retirement age, which is not only unreasonable but also unfair to the employee.

[24] *The Labor Contract Law*, Article 2.

1.3.2.3 Excluding Post-Retirement Age Workers from Labor Law Protection Might Be Seen as Age or Gender Discrimination

In recent years, age discrimination has become legally prohibited in many countries and regions. In 2000, the European Council adopted Council Directive 2000/78/EC *Establishing a General Framework for Equal Treatment in Employment and Occupation,* which prohibits discrimination on the grounds of religion or belief, disability, age, or sexual orientation in employment and occupation in Member States.[25] In the United States (U.S.) *The Age Discrimination in Employment Act* was adopted in 1967. The Act prohibited age discrimination against individuals between the ages of 40 to 65; then in 1978, the age limit was raised to 70, and further amendment in 1986 eliminated the age limit ceiling entirely.[26] The Amendments of the Act now provide protection to any employee or job seeker over the age of 40 from being discriminated against in employment and there is no upper age limit. In theory, if post-retirement age workers are excluded from labor law application it might constitute unfair treatment or discrimination against this group, which does not comply with the principle of equality.

Excluding post-retirement age workers from labor law protection may also raise issues of gender discrimination. The current retirement age in China is 60 for men, 55 for woman officials, and 50 for woman workers. Hence there exists employment treatment disparity for male and female workers between the ages of 50 and 60. Male workers between 50 and 60 automatically fall under labor law protection because they have not reached the legal retirement age, whereas female workers between the ages of 50 and 60 who have reached retirement age will not be able to establish a labor relationship if re-employed and will not be protected by labor law. This might constitute gender discrimination.

1.3.2.4 Including Post-Retirement Age Workers Under the Labor Law Protection Is Conducive to Safeguarding the Rights of the Aged

Because of the large population, there are a huge number of post-retirement age workers in China. If they are not included in labor law protections it is not only unfair for the aged but it also will make it harder to safeguard their basic rights. Labor law is a comprehensive system involving work hours, rest and holiday, minimum wage, overtime limits, safety and health, job training, social security benefits, and labor dispute resolutions. The comprehensive system provides strong protection to the physical and mental health of employees, important aspects of their basic rights, interests, and dignity. Older post-retirement age worker needs more and special physical and mental health protection due to their age, especially in terms of

[25] Article 1, Council Directive 2000/78, Establishing a General Framework for Equal Treatment in Employment and Occupation.

[26] Mark A. Rothstein, Charles B. Craver, Elinor P. Schroeder, Elaine W. Shoben, *Employment Law*, West, 2005, pp. 278–279.

work hours, overtime limits, and safety and health. If labor law is not applicable to older post-retirement age workers, it will have an extremely adverse impact on the basic rights of the aged employees.

1.3.2.5 Including Post-Retirement Age Workers Under Labor Law Protection Will Not Affect Employment of the Young

Although including post-retirement age workers under the labor law and enhancing the protection of the aged employees will be an incentive to their seeking employment, it will not necessarily affect employment of the young. On the contrast, if including post-retirement age workers under labor law protection, it will increase the labor costs of the employer, and the employer will be less willing to hire them, which is beneficial to employment of the young. If post-retirement age workers are not included in the labor law, it will lower the employer's labor costs, the employer will tend to hire more of them, and this will be less favorable to youth employment. Survey statistics from 91 countries and regions indicate that there is no positive relationship between the retirement age and the unemployment rate, and there is no evidence to support the view that in the long run raising the retirement age will lead to increased unemployment.[27] Similarly, to include post-retirement age workers under labor law protection will not affect employment of the young.

1.3.2.6 Pension Benefits and Income from Re-employment Could Be Coordinated

Some scholars' opposition to labor law's application to post-retirement age workers is based on the argument that they are already enjoying pension benefits and therefore have no need for labor law protection. This view is debatable, since the determination of a labor relationship involves an objective standard not subject to the pre-condition of whether one is enjoying pension benefits.

Extending labor law protection to post-retirement age workers may give rise to two issues: how to coordinate pension benefits and extra income from re-employment, and whether post-retirement age workers can continue to participate in and pay for social insurance program. These issues, however, can be dealt with. In some countries, retirees' pension benefits will be reduced if they have extra income from re-employment. In some countries, re-employment after retirement age will not affect retirees' pension benefits. Such a system is in place in the United Kingdom (U.K.). If the participants in the national basic pension program continue to work after retirement age, they are still entitled to a pension without

---

[27] Ming Fan, et al., *Acts of Retirement and Policies of Retirement,* Social Sciences Academic Press, 2008, pp. 236–237.

any reduction.[28] In some countries, the retirees will pay more tax if they have both pension and extra income from re-employment. So pension benefits and extra income from re-employment are not necessarily mutually exclusive, and can be handled properly.

From the above, we can see that the retirement age should not be a limiting condition for establishing a labor relationship. Reaching retirement age should not lead an employee to lose such a qualification and thus become ineligible for labor law protection. The criteria for determining a labor relationship should rely on the factual relationship of the contractual parties; retirement age should not mean the ending of a labor relationship or termination of a labor contract. Making retirement age a qualifying condition for establishing a labor relationship is a theoretical misunderstanding and a misreading of the legal implication of "retirement." And in reality it is harmful to the rights and interests of the aged employees. The term "retirement" should mean that those who have reached the retirement age can choose not to work but enjoy pension benefits. And if they choose to continue to work, their rights to be protected by labor law should not be affected.

1.3.3 Student "Employees"

In China today, large numbers of college students work in internships. Are these interns employees? In judicial practice, the majority of cases show that arbitration agencies or the courts do not accord interns the status of an "employee." Yet in some recent cases, according to the actual situation, arbitration agencies or the court may recognize interns as employees and their relationship with the employer as a labor relationship. In theory, if a student is not a mere intern but in fact replaces a regular employee of the employer, the student complies with the employer's rules and regulations and works for a relatively long period of time, and the employer pays a considerable wage, the student should be recognized as an "employee" and be protected by the labor law.

1.3.4 Apprentice

In the United Kingdom, an apprenticeship contract is regarded as one type of employment contract.[29] But China's Supreme People's Court has released a judicial interpretation stipulating that "the dispute between an individual craftsman and the

---

[28] Jianding Ding & Fengjuan Yang, *The Development of the Social Security System of the United Kingdom,* China Labor and Social Security Press, 2004, p. 192.

[29] *Employment Rights Act* 1996, s. 230(2).

apprentice" does not fall into the category of a labor dispute.[30] Yet in judicial practice the court may decide that a labor relationship did exist between a commercially registered individual craftsman and an apprentice.[31] If an apprentice only receives training, then the apprentice should not be recognized as an employee, which will give incentives to individual craftsmen providing training to apprentices without being overburdened. But if an apprentice performs the same job duties as other employees, then that apprentice should be recognized as an "employee."

1.3.5 Corporate Executives

Although the key aspect of being an employee is subordinate status, and most corporate executives are in a position of managing or controlling employees, an employer's corporate executives also comply with the definition of employees and are accorded employee status. But since corporate executives are not regular employees, in some countries, some labor law provisions do not apply to executives. For example, in the United States, white-collar employees are not under the protection of minimum wage rules and overtime compensation under certain circumstances.[32] Relevant Chinese labor law and labor contract law includes company executives as employees. For instance, the law provides that non-competition restrictions only apply to high-level executives, high-level technicians, and other personnel with confidentiality obligations.[33] Thus, it can be inferred that employees governed by the labor law include high-level executives. But legislation in China has not paid sufficient attention to the special status of executives and there is no special rule for them. This lack of regulation is a deficiency in legislation as well as in practice.

In fact, there are different types of corporate executives in a company. Members of the board of directors and board of supervisors are appointed by the shareholders and in the policy-making body, and are therefore in a position of hiring and firing high-level management and exercising control over them. From this perspective, members of the board do not fit into the definition of employees. For those managers appointed by the board of directors, although they are in high position, they are subject to the decision of the board and controlled by the board; therefore, the definition of employees does apply to such managers. For the managers, although they are still employees, because of their special responsibility and appointment and

[30] *The Interpretation of Applicable Laws in Adjudicating Labor Disputes of the Supreme People's Court* (II), 2006, Article 7.

[31] Hua Zhu, *Is There a Labor Relationship between the Individually-owned Business and the Apprentice?*; Qianli Ma, *How to Distinguish a Service Relationship and A Labor Relationship,* in *Analysis of New Difficult Labor Dispute Cases,* edited by Beijing Labor and Social Security Law Society, Law Press, 2007, pp. 3–8.

[32] Mark A. Rothstein, Charles B. Craver, Elinor P. Schroeder, Elaine W. Shoben, Employment Law, West, 2005, p. 342.

[33] *Labor Contract Law,* Article 24.

removal procedure, it is difficult to apply some labor law rules to them, such as the rules concerning overtime pay, termination. As a result, special rules regarding overtime pay, termination and other issues should be created for the corporate executives.

1.4 Establishment of a Labor Relationship

According to the *Labor Contract Law*, the employer shall sign a written labor contract with the employee when they establish a labor relationship (Article 10). If no such contract is signed between the second and the twelfth month of employment, the employer shall pay the employee double their monthly salary forth is period (Article 82); In case no written contract is signed after expiration of one year, besides the double monthly salary to be paid, it is deemed the employer has entered into "non-fixed-term" contract with the employee (Article 14). Why does the law impose such strict obligation and liability on employers in signing written contracts? This strict rule is mainly because of that, in the absence of a written contract, the employees would be very vulnerable and it would be difficult for them to receive compensation once disputes occur. According to a survey conducted by the Standing Committee of the National People's Congress (NPC) in 2005, less than 20 % of workers in medium and small-sized enterprises and non-public enterprises had written contracts, with an even lower ratio in individually-owned businesses.[34] Because of the real situation before the adoption of *Labor Contract Law*, the law imposes strict obligation and liability on the employers. In recent years, the ratio of employment relationship with written contracts has increased significantly. According to statistics by the Ministry of Human Resources and Social Security, by the end of 2013, 88.2 % of the enterprises signed written contracts with their employees.[35] It seems that the strict rule has been effective in forcing employers to sign written contracts with their employees. Although the law has strict provision on written contracts, if the parties fail to sign one, the labor relationship can also be established based on the criteria of labor relationship discussed above.

As for the term of the contract, under the *Labor Contract Law*, there are basically two types of contracts, fix-term contracts and non-fixed-term contracts. Before the adoption of the *Labor Contract Law*, there was no limit on the term of labor contracts. As a result, short-term employment was favored by employers over long-term contracts, and most employees were forced to sign short-term contracts with their employers. According to an investigation of the Standing Committee of the NPC before the adoption of the *Labor Contract Law*, more than 60 % of employers

[34] Jingyu Yang (Director of the Legal Committee of the National People's Congress), "Understanding the Labor Contract Law", July 23, 2007, available at http://news.xinhuanet.com/legal/2007-07/23/content_6418697.htm.

[35] Ministry of Human Resources and Social Security of the People's Republic of China, *Bulletin of Statistics for the Development of Human Resources and Social Security in China of 2013.*

signed contracts of one year or less with employees. This gave employers more freedom to select new employees when the contracts expired and allowed them to terminate unilaterally the employment relationship with impunity. The prevalence of short-term employment was a big concern of the legislature. In the views of the legislators, short-term employment undermined the stability of labor relations as employers were generally not willing to provide adequate training to employees or invested in the short-term employees and at the same time, the employees might also lack the incentive to achieve long-term goals because of job insecurity.[36] Against this background, *Labor Contract Law* also requires employers to sign long-term contracts with the employee. In some situations, if the employee requests to conclude a non-fixed-term labor contract, the employer is obligated to sign such contracts, when: (a) The employee has been working for no less than 10 years for the employer; (b) Fixed-term employment contracts have been concluded for two consecutive times; and other situations (Art 14). The main purpose of this rule is to increase the stability and security of labor relations. After this law, more long-term contracts had been made, but unfortunately, there are no national statistics on the duration of the labor contracts.

1.5 Qualifications for "Employer" Status and Differential Treatment for Different Types of Employers

1.5.1 Can a Natural Person Be an Employer?

According to Article 2 of the *Labor Contract Law,* only enterprises, individually-owned businesses, and private non-enterprise entities are qualified to be employers, but an individual cannot be an employer. In some countries and regions, however, an individual can be an employer. Considering that in China labor law legislation and practice are not well developed yet, at the present stage great caution should be exercised in expanding the scope of "employer." "Labor law in China is still in the development stage, there exist many defects in basic employment relationships. At present if a natural person is allowed to qualify as an employer in the sense of labor law, it will make immature labor law theory even harder to handle."[37] I agree with this argument. Adding natural persons to the "employer" category will greatly increase the number of labor relationships. Also, many current labor law rules are not fully applicable to natural person employers. At present therefore it is premature to expand the "employer" to include natural persons.

[36] Jingyu Yang (Director of the Legal Committee of the National People's Congress), "Understanding the Labor Contract Law", July 23, 2007, available at http://news.xinhuanet.com/legal/2007-07/23/content_6418697.htm.

[37] Shangyuan Zheng, *The System and Concepts of the Labor Contract Law,* China University of Political Science and Law Press, 2008, p. 66.

Expanding the scope of “employer,” however, is a developing trend that cannot be totally ignored. At present, we can draw experience from the practice of some countries and regions. For example, treating some company executives as employers, and imposing employers’ liabilities on them might promote smooth implementation of the labor law. The current unsatisfactory labor law implementation has a lot to do with the situation where the liability of illegal act is limited to the company employer, without individual accountability. Under the *Labor Contract Law*, liability for illegal acts is limited to the enterprise employer and no mention is made of the individual liability of company executives. Even in situations where there is serious harm and violation of an employee’s personal rights, the law only prescribes liability for the company employer.[38] The *Labor and Social Security Inspection Regulations* also only limits liability for an employer’s illegal acts to their administrative or civil liability and not individual liability. If we can introduce the broader concept of “employer” and make company executives who have actual decision-making power over labor matters “employers” under the law, it will provide a legal basis for holding them legally accountable. This will improve enforcement of the labor law. Making an individual liable under labor law is not only justified in legal theory but also necessary in practice.

1.5.2 Differential Treatment of Different Types of Employers

For-profit organizations in China, apart from enterprises, also include individually-owned business. Under the current labor law, when a labor relationship is established between an individually-owned business and an employee, labor law is applicable to the business in the same manner as it is applicable to enterprises. The number of individually-owned business in China now far exceeds that of enterprises. By the end of 2013, China had 15.2784 million enterprises, yet the number of individually-owned business stood at 44.3629 million.[39] Actually, small enterprise and individually-owned business (hereinafter “small business”) are very different from regular enterprises. They have more of a natural person’s attributes with lower levels of organization; they are in a disadvantaged position in terms of scale, funds, management, and human resources; their needs for hiring and firing are different; and therefore, they deserve certain special preferential treatments, such as the following:

First, since most small businesses are small in scale and have limited cash flow, overly stringent labor requirements could increase their financial burden and make it difficult for them to operate. For instance, according to the statistics of the National Administration of Industry and Commerce, in 2013, the total capital of

---

[38] *Labor Contract Law,* Article 88.

[39] *The National Major Market Development Report (2013),* by China Administration of Industry and Commerce, http://www.saic.gov.cn/zwgk/tjzl/zhtj/bgt/201401/P020140114489778954994.pdf.

individually-owned businesses stood at 2.43 trillion yuan (Chinese Yuan Renminbi, CNY),[40] with an average of only 54,800 yuan in capital for each business. Therefore, small businesses have to be more careful with cost control, especially in employee training and personnel management. They also have limited cash flow and an inadequate ability to manage risk, including risks in hiring and firing. Therefore, it would be unfair to apply labor law to small business in the same way as large enterprises and require them to comply with to the same obligations when there exists such a huge gap in scales and funds between different employers. This is especially true because many small businesses lack experience and run on small capital funds, and face great market risks. It is therefore hard for them to completely comply with labor law rules.

Yet private enterprises, including small enterprises and individually-owned businesses, are the main driving force of the market and constitute a huge bulk of the employment population. This is supported by a statistics from 2013. In 2013, newly established private enterprises and individually-owned businesses accounted for 96 % of the newly established market business. By the end of 2013, employees working in private enterprises and individually-owned businesses reached 143.8459 million, a 9.09 % increase over the year before, accounting for 40 % of the urban and rural working population. In 2013, the work force in newly established private enterprises and individually-owned business accounted for 90 % of new jobs in the country.[41] Therefore, creating a more relaxed business environment for these employers will be highly conducive to promoting business and employment.

Second, small businesses need more flexible mechanisms for hiring and firing. Due to the facts that small businesses are smaller in scale, with fewer job positions, weaker risk resistance, and lower profit margins, they need more employment flexibility, especially when hiring and firing according to market fluctuation and their own business situation. The *Labor Contract Law* outlines a relatively strict mechanism for dismissal. This could be a serious burden for small businesses of minimal scale and few employees. For example, according to *Labor Contract Law*, the employer can terminate a contract if the employee committed serious violation(s) of the workplace rules.[42] But many small businesses do not have detailed workplace rules or the rules are not clear or specific, so it can be difficult for the employer to ascertain whether the employee is in "serious violation of the workplace rules" and to have their contract terminated according to the law. Another example, according to the *Labor Contract Law*, is an employee can be legally dismissed when the employee is incompetent in their job duties and after training, or an adjustment to

[40] *The 2013 Analysis of the National Major Market Development*, by China Administration of Industry and Commerce, http://www.saic.gov.cn/zwgk/tjzl/zhtj/xxzx/201402/P020140227616783687760.pdf.

[41] *The 2013 Analysis of the National Major Market Development*, by China Administration of Industry and Commerce, http://www.saic.gov.cn/zwgk/tjzl/zhtj/xxzx/201402/P020140227616783687760.pdf.

[42] *Labor Contract Law*, Article 39, Sec. 2.

the employee's position, the employee still cannot perform his job duties.[43] As small businesses, especially individually-owned business may have little or no training capacity and limited and few job positions, it is hard for business owners to provide training or to adjust the employee's position, and therefore it is also hard to terminate the contract. On the contrary, large enterprises can employ detailed workplace rules crafted by professionals and have many job positions and sufficient training capacity. Thus, they can make full use of the legitimate reasons allowed under the *Labor Contract Law* to dismiss employees.

If small enterprises or individually-owned business with few employees cannot hire and fire employees in a timely manner it will have large adverse effect on their business and profits. Especially for very small individually-owned business, even adding or reducing one employee can have a profound impact. Actually, most individually-owned businesses have few employees. According to the statistics of the National Administration of Industry and Commerce, in the first quarter of 2009, there were 6.6427 million private enterprises (including branches) with a labor force of 62.9616 million employees.[44] Thus the average number of employees for each private business is less than 10. As for individually-owned business, there were 29.48 million of them by March 2009 with 58.0953 million employees,[45] averaging less than 2 workers per business. As a result, adding or reducing even one employee will have a direct impact on business and profits of individually-owned business. Therefore, small businesses have a greater need for freedom in hiring and especially in firing matters.

Yet minor fluctuations in the number of employees will have little impact on large enterprises with a large number of employees. Hence it is evident that the contract termination rule of the current *Labor Contract Law* is not beneficial to small businesses. It is not fair to apply the same dismissal rules to large and small businesses alike. This will cause too heavy a burden on some small businesses.

Third, many small businesses have limited human resources and are lacking in professional and legal knowledge. It is difficult for them to comply with the labor law and related regulations strictly. They usually do not have a professional human resource manager, whereas large-scale enterprises have professional management and human resource teams. Thus, it seems unfair to require that small businesses comply with the same labor law, and shoulder the same liability as big enterprises. For instance, many small business owners are not aware that a written labor contract must be signed or they face liability to pay double the wage.[46] Now, labor laws and labor-

---

[43] *Labor Contract Law*, Article 40, Sec. 2.

[44] *Statistics and Analysis Release: The National Major Market Development Report, First Quarter of 2009*, by China Administration of Industry and Commerce, http://www.saic.gov.cn/zwgk/tjzl/zhtj/bgt/200905/t20090511_47153.html.

[45] *Statistics and Analysis Release: The National Major Market Development Report, First Quarter of 2009*, by the General Office of China Administration of Industry and Commerce, http://www.saic.gov.cn/zwgk/tjzl/zhtj/bgt/200905/t20090511_47153.html.

[46] *Labor Contract Law*, Article 10, 14, 82.

related social security and relevant laws and policies are getting more complex, which makes it more difficult, for small business owners to achieve full compliance.

Fourth, in small businesses, the employee and employer often have a special relationship, making it difficult to fully apply labor law rules, or that following the legal requirements fully would be against customs and cultural traditions. For example, many small business owners like to hire relatives, friends, or fellow villagers. There is a lot of trust involved and the labor relationship is often governed through such trust rather than legal rules. For example, requiring a written contract with clear stipulations of all matters in advance seems unreasonable. Fifth, some rules in the *Labor Law* and *Labor Contract Law* are hard for small businesses to implement. For example, the *Labor Contract Law* stipulates that when an employer unilaterally terminates a labor contract the employer should notify the trade union of the reason for dismissal; if the employer has violated the law, administrative regulations, or the labor contract, the trade union has the subsequent right to ask the employer to make corrections.[47] In reality, most small businesses do not have a trade union, which has caused many disputes over the application of this provision in situations of contract termination. Also, the *Labor Contract Law* stipulates that if an employee has worked for ten years for an employer, or if two consecutive fixed-term labor contracts have been signed, the employee has the right to ask for a non-fixed-term contract. Again, in reality, most small businesses do not last very long. Many small businesses do not last very long because they are small in size, have low levels of investment, and need to close down or make adjustments according to market situation. Therefore, there is little room to apply the non-fixed-term contract rules in the *Labor Contract Law* to small businesses.

1.5.3 How to Provide Differential Treatment

It is therefore necessary to give certain special and preferential labor law treatment to small businesses to reduce their burden and to promote employment. Some countries have rules like this. For example, although Germany has a very strict dismissal protection requiring employers to have legitimate reasons for and to follow due process when dismissing employees, Germany's *Protection Against Unfair Dismissal Act* is not applicable to employers with fewer than 10 employees. The legislative intent of this exemption is to help small businesses create more employment. The legislature believes that if there is more flexibility in the employer-employee relationship, the employer will be more likely to hire workers.[48] In the United States some labor law rules also accord small businesses some exemptions. For example, Title VII of the *Civil Rights Act* of 1964 prohibits discrimination by

---

[47] *Labor Contract Law*, Article 43.

[48] Roger Blanpain, Susan Bison-Rapp, William R. Corbett, Hilary K. Josephs, and Michael Zimmer, *The Global Workplace: the International and Comparative Employment Law-Cases and Materials*, Cambridge University Press, 2007, p. 400.

the employer on the basis of race, color, religion, gender or nationality, but it is only applicable to employers that have more than 15 employees.[49] And the *Age Discrimination in Employment Act* of 1967 prohibits discrimination in employment against individuals over the age of 40, but it is only applicable to employers that have more than 20 employees.[50] The *Americans with Disabilities Act* of 1990 is the primary piece of legislation to protect people with disabilities in employment; it is also only applicable to employers that have more than 15 employees.[51] All this anti-discrimination legislation is not applicable to employers with employees less than certain numbers. The legislative intent of Congress was not to overburden small businesses with federal laws. Labor law waivers for small businesses in Korea are even more comprehensive. Korea's most important labor law legislation, the *Labor Standards Act*, is only applicable to enterprises or employers that employ 5 or more workers at all times, and it is neither applicable to domestic workers nor to enterprises or employers that only employ relatives who live together.[52] This actually excludes small businesses and family business from application of the law. At the same time, according the Korean President's Order, certain provisions of the law can be applicable to enterprises or employers that have four or less workers.[53]

Based on the above, in the future, China could draw on the experience of other countries and give preferential treatment to small enterprises and individually-owned businesses in regards to written contracts, grounds and process for labor contract termination, formulation of workplace rules, and so on, so as to allow these entities more freedom in employment.[54]

---

[49] Section 701(b), Title VII of the Civil Rights Act of 1964.

[50] Section 11(b), The Age Discrimination in Employment Act of 1967.

[51] Section 101(5), The Americans with Disabilities Act of 1990.

[52] Korea *Labor Standards Law,* English ed., 1997, Article 10.

[53] Korea *Labor Standards Law,* English ed., 1997, Article 10.

[54] Zengyi Xie, *Legislation Should Avoid "One Size Fits All" Approach,* Finance and Economics, 2008, No. 8, p. 68.

Chapter 2
Basic Duties of the Employer and the Employee

A labor relationship in the form of a pay-for-labor service contract has attributes of a contract under private law and also elements of public interest. As a regular contract under civil law, the core of a labor contract is the basic rights and duties of the parties. A labor relationship concerns not only economic interests but also personal interests, so it involves both private and public interest factors, which makes the parties' rights and duties in a labor contract more complex. In any labor contract, in addition to the employee's duty to provide labor service and the employer's duty to pay for the labor service delivered, due to the personal nature of the two parties in the relationship, it also contains a series of other related duties. The study of the parties' basic rights and duties in a labor contract is necessary because the law cannot clearly prescribe all the specific rights and duties of the parties. Additionally, it is difficult for the parties to specify in the contract each other's rights and duties down to the last detail. Therefore, the understanding of the basic rights and duties of the parties will enable smooth performance of the labor contract, and to provide legal base when the parties seek legal remedy.

2.1 Basic Duties of the Employer and the Employee in Labor Law

According to the provisions of *Labor Law*, rights enjoyed by the employee include: the right to equal opportunity in employment and choice of occupation, right to remuneration for labor delivered; right to rest and holiday leave, right to workplace safety and health protection, right to vocational training, right to social security and related benefits, right to labor dispute resolution; and other labor related rights prescribed by law. Duties of the employee include: the duty to perform one's job duties, the duty to improve one's occupational skills, the duty to comply with workplace safety and health rules, and the duty to abide by workplace disciplinary rules and

Z. Xie, *Labor Law in China*, Research Series on the Chinese Dream and China's Development Path, DOI 10.1007/978-3-662-46929-3_2

professional codes of conduct.[1] Given the correspondence relation between rights and duties, we can infer on the basis of the rights of the employee that duties of the employer include those to treat all employees equally, to pay employees for work done, to allow rest and holiday leave, workplace safety and health protection measures, vocational training, and social security and related benefits. The *Labor Contract Law* does not have specific provisions of the contracting parties' basic rights and duties. Even though the *Labor Law* has provisions for the rights and duties of the employee, this is not sufficient for judicial practice.

What the basic rights and duties of the employer and employee are remains a theoretical subject that needs further study. Since *Labor Law* in China is relatively vague and broad, studying legislation and case law from other countries can be beneficial.

2.2 Duties of the Employer and the Employee in Some Countries

2.2.1 Duties of the Employer and Employee Under the Laws in Germany

In Germany, which is typical of countries within the continental legal tradition, employment contract is partly governed by the civil codes. And the duties of the employer and employee are greatly influenced by contract law theory, especially the theory of primary duties and collateral obligations. In summary, the duties of the employee under German law include: (1) duty to work; (2) ancillary duties, which includes the duty to be loyal and special ancillary duties such as notice and reporting, loss reduction, confidentiality, restriction on freedom of speech, prohibition on accepting bribes, and non-competition.[2] The employer has the following four main duties: (1) the duty to pay remuneration; (2) ancillary duties such as those to care for the employee and special ancillary duties such as those to protect employee's life, health, personal dignity, and personal properties such as they might carry; (3) the duty to provide expense indemnification; and (4) the duty to employ the employee.[3]

The basic duties of the employer and employee under German law mainly come from the theory of contracts. But the ancillary duties of the employer mainly come from special laws. This is due to the fact that, in Germany, a labor contract is treated as a private law contract.[4] In general, in Germany, the duties of the employer and employee are governed by the Civil Codes, contract law, and special labor laws.

[1] *Labor Law*, Article 3.

[2] Wilhelm Dutz, *Labor Law*, Guowen Zhang trans., Law Press, 2005, pp. 58–65.

[3] Wilhelm Dutz, *Labor Law*, Guowen Zhang trans., Law Press, 2005, pp. 65–75.

[4] Wilhelm Dutz, *Labor Law*, Guowen Zhang trans., Law Press, 2005, p. 16.

2.2.2 Duties of the Employer and Employee Under the Laws in the U.K.

The United Kingdom, a typical country in the common law tradition, has a contract theory that is very different from those adopted by countries in the continental legal tradition. Duties in a contract generally are either express or implied obligations. If the court deems that the parties did not include certain important provisions in a labor contract, the court can include these provisions in the contract as implied obligations.[5] Apart from implied obligations, the parties can include all clauses of their negotiated agreement in the contract; however, the terms of an agreement between the parties are still subject to strict restrictions of statutes.[6] Interpretations of British laws primarily treat a labor contract as a personal contract where the parties have obligations to provide personal service to each other.[7]

In the U.K., the basic duties of the employer and employee are mainly implied obligations that originate from common law principles; however, they are also influenced by statutes.

2.2.2.1 Duties of the Employer

According to the laws of the U.K., the employer's duties mainly include: (1) the duty to provide work,(2) the duty to pay wages, (3) the duty to indemnify, (4) the duty in relation to references, (5) the duty of mutual respect/trust and confidence, and (6) the duty to ensure the employee's safety.[8] Previously, case law in the U.K. did not recognize the employer's duty to provide work for the employee. But the courts have gradually come to recognize that having work to do and getting paid are equally important for employees. So under some circumstances the employer has the duty to provide work to the employee. As for reference, unless it is clearly stated in the contract, the employer usually has no obligation to provide references for the employee. But in reality, most employers will do so. If the employer chooses to do so, they are to some measure responsible for the content of the reference. The duty of mutual respect is applicable to both the employer and the employee. This obligation is most relevant in unfair dismissal.

2.2.2.2 Duties of the Employee

According to the laws of the U.K., the employee's duties mainly include (1) the duty of cooperation. In the U.K., the law requires that the employee serves the employer faithfully and acts in a loyal manner. The U.K. also requires the employee to comply

---

[5] Deborah J Lockton, *Employment Law*, 5th Edition, Palgrave Macmillan, 2006, p. 56.

[6] Deborah J Lockton, *Employment Law*, 5th Edition, Palgrave Macmillan, 2006, pp. 35–36.

[7] Deborah J Lockton, *Employment Law*, 5th Edition, Palgrave Macmillan, 2006, p. 56.

[8] Deborah J Lockton, *Employment Law*, 5th Edition, Palgrave Macmillan, 2006, pp. 58–76.

with (2) the duty to obey reasonable lawful order. Obeying the employer's instructions is the most basic duty of the employee. Other duties of the employee include: (3) the duty to exercise reasonable care and skill; (4) the duty not to accept bribes or secret commissions; (5) the duty not to disclose confidential information; and (6) the duty not to work for a competitor.[9]

From the legislation and cases of Germany and the U.K., we can see there are similarities as well as differences between the two countries in regard to the duties of the employer and employee. Laws in both countries have provisions for duties of loyalty of the employee toward the employer, including confidentiality, not to accept bribes, and not to compete. The employer also has similar duties such as those to pay wages, to provide work, to indemnify expenses, and to ensure the employee's safety and health.

2.3 Factors that Determine the Duties of the Employer and the Employee

To determine the duties of the employer and employee by law, several factors need to be taken into consideration, such as the contents of the contract, the nature of a labor relationship, and the purpose of labor law.

To be more specific, first, the content and purpose of a contract need to be examined. In a labor contract, the employee offers the labor expected by the employer to earn a wage. Therefore, the employer has the duty to provide work and to disburse remuneration. Correspondingly, the employee has the duty to provide the labor expected by the employer. Since the employee only provides labor service, and often times the employer's property is in the hands of the employee, and the employer shoulders the risks in running the business, the employee has a duty of care and loyalty, and other than for wage remuneration, cannot sacrifice the employer's interest to further their own. While at work the employee must contemplate and safeguard the employer's interests in ways expected by the employer.

Second, the personal nature of a labor contract needs to be examined. The employee usually must work at the site provided by the employer and accept the employer's command and control. When a labor contract covers a long period of time, the parties cannot cover all the details by agreement in the contract, and the content of work may change with market conditions, advances in technology, and the employer's business situation. This makes cooperation and trust between the parties crucial. Therefore, both the employer and the employee should bear a duty of mutual respect and trust.

Third, the subordination of the employee to the employer and the imbalance between their respective statuses need to be examined. The employer often makes rules and gives instructions that the employee must obey. Yet the employer cannot

[9] Deborah J Lockton, *Employment Law*, 5th Edition, Palgrave Macmillan, 2006, pp. 102–112.

abuse this power, and the rules and instructions must be lawful and reasonable. Since the employee must work at the site provided by the employer, the employer has the duty to care for and protect the employee. This duty covers safety, health, vocational training, rest and holiday leave, and other issues.

2.4 Improvement of Duties of the Employer and the Employee

From the comparative perspective, Chinese labor laws need further improvement regarding the duties of the employee and the employer.

2.4.1 The Employee's Duties of Due Diligence and Loyalty

2.4.1.1 The Employee's Duty of Due Diligence

Article 3 section 2 of the *Labor Law* stipulates "the employee should complete job duties, improve vocational skills, observe workplace safety and health rules, and abide by workplace discipline and professional codes of conduct." This duty, apart from that to "abide by professional codes of conduct," mainly concerns the duty of due diligence. This provision needs to be improved. "Completing job duties" is inherent in the labor contract and an imperative for the employee. "Improving vocational skills" is part of the duty of due diligence and overly broad. In the course of performance of a labor contract, the employee's duty should be a "duty to exercise reasonable care and skill." The degree of "care" and appropriate "skill" should be determined by the specific work situation. The duty to "improve vocational skills" is too general.

According to the *Labor Law* and *Labor Contract Law*, the employee has the duty to observe workplace safety and health rules, workplace discipline, and other workplace rules. And the *Labor Contract Law* requires that the content of the workplace rules must be legal.[10] The making of workplace rules also must be in compliance with statutory procedure. Under the *Labor Contract Law*, when the employer makes or modifies workplace rules, or decides significant matters that will have a direct impact on vital interests of the employees, such as wage remuneration, work time, rest and holiday leave, workplace safety and health, insurance benefits, vocational training, workplace discipline, and output quota, the matters should be submitted to

---

[10] *Labor Contract Law* Article 80 states: "If the rules of the employer directly affect the employee's vital interests and the rules violate provisions of laws or regulations, the labor administrative agency can issue order of correction and warning; if the violation caused harm for the employee, the employer is liable for damages." Therefore the law only requires that the rules are legal but not necessarily reasonable.

the workers assembly or all the workers for discussion and proposals. The matters should then be decided through equal consultation with the trade union or workers' representatives, and made public and known to the workers.[11] Any workplace rules made in violation of the statutory procedure have no binding effect over the employees.

Although China's labor law provisions stipulate that the content of workplace rules must be legal, it does not stipulate that the content should also be reasonable. This is a defect. In theory, the employee only has a duty to observe legal and reasonable workplace rules. The employee has no obligation to observe rules or regulations that are illegal or unreasonable. However, whether the court should have the discretion to decide whether a workplace rule is reasonable still debatable in practice.

2.4.1.2 The Employee's Duty of Loyalty

(1) Observing professional codes of conduct

For the duty of loyalty, the *Labor Law* has one general provision stating that the employee should observe "professional code of conduct."[12] An elastic concept, "professional code of conduct" here emphasizes that the employee should work in good faith, observe common trade practice, and consider and safeguard the employer's interests. This duty can make up for legislative deficiency. In judicial practice, when the employee's conduct causes harm to the interest of the employer, the court should be allowed to use the rule of duty of loyalty to hold the employee liable.

(2) Duties of confidentiality and non-competition

As those in many other countries, China's *Labor Contract Law* also has provisions governing the employee's duties of confidentiality and non-competition, which stipulate that the employer and the employee can make agreements in the labor contract for safeguarding the employer's trade secrets and other confidential information regarding intellectual property.[13] Confidentiality should be one of the basic duties of the employee; even when there is no such agreement in the contract, the employee still has this duty.

Article 23 section 2 of the *Labor Contract Law* is the competition restriction provision, which stipulates that "for those employees who have a duty of confidentiality, the employer can have a non-competition agreement with the employee in the labor contract or in a separate confidentiality agreement which stipulates that upon dissolution or termination of the labor contract, the employee will be compensated on a monthly basis for the period of non-competition. If the employee

[11] *Labor Contract Law*, Article 4.

[12] *Labor Contract Law*, Article 3.

[13] *Labor Contract Law*, Article 23.

violates the non-competition agreement, the employee should pay the employer agreed damages for breaching the contract."

This provision has many ambiguities that make implementation difficult. If there is a non-competition clause in the agreement between the employer and the employee that does not specify the amount of compensation, is the non-competition clause still valid? No answer can be found in the law or judicial interpretations of the Supreme People's Court. Some scholars hold that according to the principles of fairness and reasonableness, if there is no monetary compensation clause, the non-competition agreement should be considered invalid.[14] But according to one judicial interpretation of the Supreme People's Court, if there is a non-competition clause without mention of specific monetary compensation, and the employee fulfilled the non-competition duty, the employer should pay the employee in the amount of 30 % of average monthly salary for the 12-month period that ended immediately before the dissolution or termination of the employment contract.[15] The question is whether the non-competition clause is still valid if there is a non-competition clause without mention of specific monetary compensation, and the employee doesn't fulfill the non-competition duty. This remains unanswered.

The law has no specific provision for the amount of "monetary compensation." As long as there is an agreement of non-competition and monetary compensation, when the parties end the labor contract, if the employer requires the employee to fulfill the non-competition duty or if the employee has done so and requests the employer to pay compensation for doing so, the court will usually support the employee.[16]

The outcome of the non-competition agreement when one party fails to fulfill the duty is also a complex issue. If there is an agreement of non-competition and compensation, and the employer fails to pay the compensation in a timely manner. What recourse is available to the employees? According to the judicial interpretation of the Supreme People's Court, "If the employer does not pay the compensation for three months, and the employee requests that the non-competition clause be terminated, the request should be supported by the court."[17] Thus when the employer fails to pay the compensation for a considerable period of time, which constitutes a serious breach, the employee can terminate the agreement. Under this rule, if non-payment persists for less than three months, then the employee can only request that the employer pay the compensation but not the termination of the agreement.

What if the employer requests an early termination of the agreement within the agreed time period of non-competition? The judicial interpretation of the Supreme

[14] Xiong Li, *Four Points of Determining the Validity of a Non-Competition Agreement,* Law Application, 2013, No. 1, p. 59.

[15] *The Interpretation of Applicable Laws in Adjudicating Labor Disputes of the Supreme People's Court* (IV), 2012, Article 6.

[16] *The Interpretation of Applicable Laws in Adjudicating Labor Disputes of the Supreme People's Court* (IV), 2012, Article 7.

[17] *The Interpretation of Applicable Laws in Adjudicating Labor Disputes of the Supreme People's Court* (IV), 2012, Article 8.

People's Court states that under this circumstance the court should support the employer's request. And when the non-competition agreement is terminated and the employee requests that the employer pay extra compensation for three months, the court should support such a request.[18] Therefore, the court allows an early termination of the non-competition agreement by the employer provided they pay the employee extra compensation. Since early termination of the non-competition agreement will liberate the employee from the obligation of non-competition and the employers from the obligation of paying compensation for the rest of the time period covered by the agreement, it is right for the court to allow early termination of the agreement by the employer. In such cases, the employer has breached the agreement, it is reasonable for the employer to pay extra compensation to the employee.

What should be done if the employee breaches the contract? The position of the court is that "if the employee breaches the non-competition agreement and pays the employer for the breach and the employer requests that the employee continue to fulfill the non-competition duty according to the agreement, the court should support such request."[19] The court's interpretation treats the employee more stringently that it does the employer. When the employee breaches the agreement, the employee must pay a penalty and continue to honor the duty of non-competition. Whereas the rules free the employer from the agreed duty as long as they pay three months extra compensation in exchange for the early termination of the agreement. The court's position seems to favor the employer and puts the employee at a disadvantage. It is unacceptable to impose a non-competition duty on the employee that excessively restricts their freedom of employment.[20] Hence the court's position is questionable.

The law also places restrictions on the scope of applicable employees and time period for non-competition. Under the *Labor Contract Law*, the non-competition duty is only applicable to senior executives, senior technicians, and other persons that have a duty of confidentiality. The applicable job scope, geographical area, and time period of non-competition shall be agreed upon between the employer and the employee and such agreement shall not be in violation of any laws or regulations. The time period of non-competition shall not be more than two years.[21] This two-year limit is appropriate since longer restrictions will affect the employee's freedom of employment and competition in the labor market.

Since a non-competition agreement is both closely connected to and independent of the labor contract, the effect of the dissolution or termination of the labor contract on the validity of non-competition agreement is quite complicated. Due to the different reasons for and means of labor contract dissolution or termination,

---

[18] *The Interpretation of Applicable Laws in Adjudicating Labor Disputes of the Supreme People's Court* (IV), 2012, Article 9.

[19] *The Interpretation of Applicable Laws in Adjudicating Labor Disputes of the Supreme People's Court* (IV), 2012, Article 10.

[20] Xiong Li, *Four Points of Determining the Validity of a Non-Competition Agreement,* Law Application, 2013, No. 1, p. 61.

[21] *Labor Contract Law,* Article 24.

neither the law nor judicial interpretations provide specific guidelines for determining such effects. This remains to be seen in future judicial practice.

Moonlighting is an issue related to non-competition issue. The *Labor Contract Law* does not prohibit moonlighting. Article 39 of the law states that the employee can establish a labor relationship with other employers simultaneously as long as it does not seriously affect its ability to fulfill the job duties of the current employer.[22] So an employee can work for multiple employers. But Article 39 section 4 of the law also states that "if the employee has simultaneous labor relationships with other employers which seriously undermine their ability to perform the job duties for a certain employer, or when the employer points it out and the employee refuses to make a correction, then the employer can terminate the contract." This provision indicates that in the case of moonlighting, a labor contract can be terminated as long as the employer expresses objection and the employee refuses to correct. Thus whether the employee can moonlight is totally up to the employer, which is unreasonable. In theory, unless moonlighting adversely affects the employee's job performance or harms the employer's interests, the employee should be allowed.

2.4.2 *Duties of the Employer*

Labor laws in China do not have clear provisions regarding duties of the employer and they can only be inferred from the rights of the employee mentioned above under the *Labor Law*. Apart from general duties of wage and safe and healthy workplace environment, the following duties of the employer should be considered and improved in China's legislation and judicial practice.

2.4.2.1 Duty to Provide Work

Article 4 of the *Labor Law* stipulates that the employer should formulate and perfect workplace rules according to law and ensure that the employee can enjoy the right to work and perform the duty to work. Article 4 of the *Labor Contract Law* has the same provision. These two provisions indicate that the employer has a duty to provide work for the employee according to the contract. Article 17 of the *Labor Contract Law* also stipulates that the content of a labor contract include "work task and work location," which also imply that providing work is the employer's duty. Therefore, in general, the employer has a duty to provide work for the employee. This is similar to legislation in other countries such as Germany and the U.K..

[22] *Labor Contract Law,* Article 39, Sec. 4 states that a labor contract can be terminated if the employee has a simultaneous labor relationship with other employer(s), which seriously affects the employee's fulfillment of the job duties of the first employer, and the employee refuses to make correction after notice given by the employer.

2.4.2.2 Duty to Indemnify

Neither the *Labor Law* nor *Labor Contract Law* has provisions on the employers' duty to indemnify. In practice, expenses incurred by the employee for the interest of the employer in the process of work usually will be borne by the employer. But problems remain as to how to deal with expenses incurred by the employee without the employer's permission, or expenses incurred by the employee during work when fulfilling job duties in an illegal way. In theory, the employer should be responsible for the expense if it is required by the employer, or needed by the work task. And if the employee is at fault, the employer can reduce the amount of indemnification.

2.4.2.3 Duty of Mutual Respect

There is no such provision under Chinese legislation. The labor relationship constitutes long-term cooperation with strong personal connections. The purpose of the employee working for the employer is not only to obtain wages but also to gain satisfaction and emotional enrichment at work. Moreover, the employee is in a subordinate position to the employer, with a duty to observe the employer's instructions and management. Therefore, the duty of mutual respect is highly necessary, especially on the part of the employer in regard to the employee. Introduction of "the duty of mutual respect" such as is contained in the British labor law into the labor laws in China could be considered. Establishing this duty could provide a legal basis for dealing with liability issues when acts of the employer or the employee have caused damage to the reputation, or personal or other interests of the other party in the absence of specific agreement in the contract.

Chapter 3
Anti-discrimination Law in the Workplace

3.1 Introduction

Equality in the workplace is an important element of the right to equality protected by China's constitution,[1] and one of the important human rights protected by international human rights covenants and legal documents.[2] In recent years, a trend has emerged in many countries' labor policies and laws: the increasing importance attached to the protection of the right to equality. For example, the European Union (EU) has adopted a series of directives concerning equal treatment in the workplace and greatly enhanced legislation and enforcement in its Member States.[3] China is not an exception to this global trend. In recent years, China has made much effort in promoting equality by ratifying the related United Nations (UN) and International

This chapter was first published with the title of "New Developments in Anti-discrimination in the workplace in China: Law and Practice" in Ulla Liukkunen and Chen Yifeng (eds.): "China and ILO Fundamental Principles and Rights at Work" (Bulletin of Comparative Labour Relations), Kluwer Law International, 2014, pp. 143–162. Few changes have been made to the original chapter when it was included in this book.

[1] Constitution of The People's Republic of China, Art. 33 (1982).

[2] Such covenants and documents include the Universal Declaration of Human Rights, GA Res. 217(III), UNGAOR, 3d Sess., Supp. No. 13, UN Doc. A/810 (1948) and the International Covenant on Economic, Social and Cultural Rights, GA Res. 2200A(XXI), UNGAOR, Supp. No. 16 at 49, UN Doc. A/6316 (1966) (hereinafter International Covenant on Economic, Social and Cultural Rights).

[3] Directives concerning equal treatment in the workplace include Council Directive No. 2000/43/EC implementing the principle of equal treatment between persons irrespective of racial or ethnic origin (29 Jun. 2000), OJ L 180, 19/07/2000 pp. 22–26; Council Directive 2000/78/EC establishing a general framework for equal treatment in employment and occupation (27 Nov. 2000), OJ L 303, 02/12/2000 pp. 16–22; and Directive 2006/54/EC of the European Parliament and of the Council on the implementation of the principle of equal opportunities and equal treatment of men and women in matters of employment and occupation (recast) (5 Jul. 2006), OJ L 204, 26/07/2006 pp. 23–36.

Z. Xie, *Labor Law in China*, Research Series on the Chinese Dream and China's Development Path, DOI 10.1007/978-3-662-46929-3_3

Labor Organization (ILO) conventions[4] and enacting domestic legislation. Ratifying the two fundamental labor international conventions on equal treatment, namely the ILO Equal Remuneration Convention, 1951 (No. 100)[5] and the ILO Discrimination (Employment and Occupation) Convention, 1958 (No. 111)[6] would impact greatly on Chinese domestic legislation and enforcement.[7] This chapter examines new developments in Chinese anti-discrimination law in recent years with a focus on progress and challenges in legislating and enforcing the law.

3.2 Current Employment Discrimination Situation and Its Origins

At present, the general awareness of equality in employment is still weak, and employment discrimination is prevalent in China. According to a recent survey directed by Professor Dingjian Cai from the China University of Political Science and Law, 54.9 % of respondents surveyed indicated that they had experienced discrimination, of which 15.6 % considered the discrimination serious.[8] A broad range of factors are considered when employers review job applicants and assess employees, according to the survey. These include factors such as gender, age, health condition, physical appearance, height, disabilities, political affiliation, registered permanent residence, and sexual orientation. Discrimination occurs during all stages of employment from application, hiring, work assignment, compensation and benefits, to the promotion and termination of employment.[9] Given this fact, China still has a long way to go in eliminating employment discrimination.

The reasons behind employment discrimination are complicated. From a psychological perspective, discrimination can be categorized into the intentional and the unintentional. This is indicated in the different rules on how to interpret 'discrimination' in different jurisdictions. For example, in the United States (US), an individual claim of intentional discrimination is known as a 'disparate treatment' claim under Title VII of the Civil Rights Act of 1964. Here, the controlling question

[4] China ratified the International Covenant on Economic, Social and Cultural Rights on 27 Mar. 2001, the ILO Convention on Equal Remuneration, 1951 (No. 100) on 2 Nov. 1990 and the ILO Convention on Discrimination (Employment and Occupation), 1958 (No. 111) on 12 Jan. 2006.

[5] Adopted 29 Jun. 1951, entry into force 23 May 1953.

[6] Adopted 25 Jun. 1958, entry into force 15 Jun. 1960.

[7] A remarkable achievement in this respect is adoption of the Employment Promotion Law, adopted 30 Aug. 2007, entry into force 1 Jan. 2008.

[8] Dingjian Cai, *Employment Discrimination in China: Current Conditions and Anti-discrimination Strategies*, China Social Science Press, 2007, p. 520. Directed by Prof. Cai, the Institution of Constitutionalism Study at the China University of Political Science and Law carried out a survey in May 2006 and October 2006, in ten cities in China. Of the 3,500 questionnaires issued, 3,454 valid answers were received. For the total survey result, see 505–547.

[9] Ibid. at 512–519.

of fact is the motivation of the employer.[10] But in some cases in other countries such as the United Kingdom (U.K.), judges have ruled that the test for discrimination is objective and therefore motive or intention is irrelevant. This rule was established in the important case of *James v. Eastleigh Borough Council* (1990) 2 AC 751.[11] In terms of the above rules and cases, prohibited discrimination could include both intentional and unintentional discrimination.

In China, the reasons for discrimination are complex. The first reason is the imbalance between the supply of labor and demand for it.[12] In China, the large supply of human labor relative to demand places employers in a more advantageous position when picking employees.[13] Cai's survey further confirms that employees believe that the basic reason for discrimination lies in the imbalance of supply and demand in the job market: 69.4 % of respondents surveyed attributed discrimination to the imbalance of the labor market.[14] Consequently, some employers impose strict or even discriminatory requirements during job recruitment.[15]

The second reason is the lack of equality consciousness or legal awareness. This is an important cause of most unconscious discrimination, although few employers may have subjective malice to discriminate. In China, legislation on anti-discrimination in employment is comparatively new and the history of legal practice in anti-discrimination is relatively short.[16] As a result, improving the equality consciousness of employers and employees is a long-term process. Weak equality consciousness is an important reason for employers often imposing unreasonable requirements as to age, sex, or even physical appearance. From the employee side, many workers in China are migrant workers who live in rural areas before they work in cities and therefore tend to be less educated. For example, in China, as mentioned earlier, migrant workers amounted to 268,940,000 in 2013.[17] The high percentage of migrant workers is an important factor for the weakness of equality awareness. Employees' overall awareness of their rights with respect to discrimination in the

[10] Mark A. Rothstein et al., *Employment Law Hornbook*, 3d ed., West, 2005, p. 123.

[11] Deborah J. Lockton, *Employment Law*, 5th ed., Palgrave Macmillan, 2006, p. 131.

[12] According to official statistics for 2007–2011, the recorded unemployment rate was 4.0–4.3 %: Ministry of Human Resources and Social Security of the People's Republic of China, *Bulletin of Statistics for the Development of Human Resources and Social Security in China* (Beijing 2011). As the unemployment rate in the Bulletin is only based on job losses registered in urban areas, the actual rate for the whole population should be higher.

[13] Jiefeng Lu, *Employment Discrimination in China: The Current Situation and Principle Challenges*, 32 Hamline L. Rev. 133, 172 (2009).

[14] Dingjian Cai, *Employment Discrimination in China: Current Conditions and Anti-discrimination Strategies*, China Social Science Press, 2007, p. 543.

[15] Ibid. at 518.

[16] The *Labor Law*, adopted 5 Jul. 1994, entry in force 1 Jan. 1995, only contains general principles of equality. The law containing more specific rules on anti-discrimination, namely the *Employment Promotion Law*, was adopted in 2007.

[17] Ministry of Human Resources and Social Security of the People's Republic of China, *Bulletin of Statistics for the Development of Human Resources and Social Security in China of 2013*.

workplace is relatively lower and they are less likely to understand when they are being unequally treated.[18]

The third reason is incorrect knowledge or attitudes on the part of employers in relation to factors such as gender, age, region and health. Traditional views held by some citizens about women, migrant workers and those with infectious diseases exacerbate unfair treatment in the workplace.[19] For example, many employers conduct mandatory Hepatitis B virus (HBV) tests and reject applicants with positive test results, mainly due to their miscomprehension of the harm of HBV.[20]

The last but not the least reason is institutional factors. For example, the 'household registration system' (*hùkǒu*) might encourage employers to prefer local (i.e., registered resident) applicants, which means non-resident applicants cannot enjoy equal opportunities in the job market. Additionally, China's employment regime was developed during a process of reform of the planned economic system which still has an impact on the job market. Due to some restrictions that still exist under the planned system, such as control of the numbers of employees in certain companies, particularly some state-owned enterprises (SOEs), some employers have to hire agency workers.[21] In addition, agency workers often suffer discrimination as a common phenomenon and there are significant differences in wages and other benefits between agency workers and those directly employed by employers.[22]

3.3 Development of China's Anti-discrimination Law in the Workplace

To date, there is no specific anti-discrimination law on the workplace in China. Provisions governing anti-discrimination in the workplace are scattered among the Constitution and other relevant labor laws, regulations and rules. For example, Article 33 of the Constitution stipulates, 'All citizens of the People's Republic of China are equal before the law.' This is the fundamental legal base for anti-discrimination legislation. The *Labor Law* of the PRC in 1994 was the first law

[18] Na Lan, *Is There New Hope in Labor Rights Protection for Chinese Migrant Workers?*, 10 Asian-Pac. L. & Pol'y J. 482, 483 (2009), quoted in Crystal Roberts, Student Author, *Far from a Harmonious Society: Employment Discrimination in China*, 52 Santa Clara L. Rev. 1531, 1556 (2012).

[19] Na Lan, ibid. at 493, quoted in Roberts, ibid. at 1555–1556.

[20] A survey by the Institute of Constitutionalism in the China University of Political Science and Law in 2006 says the most serious discrimination in people's concept is health discrimination: Dingjian Cai, *Employment Discrimination in China: Current Conditions and Anti-discrimination Strategies*, China Social Sciences Press, 2007, p. 535.

[21] The number of agency workers is usually not counted in the total number of employees of enterprises.

[22] National People's Congress of the People's Republic of China, *Explanations on Draft Amendment to the Labor Contract Law of the PRC*, in Chinese (available at http://www.npc.gov.cn/npc/xinwen/lfgz/flca/2012-07/06/content_1729107.htm) (accessed 5 Feb. 2013).

which provided general principles for anti-discrimination in China. Similarly, Article 3 of the *Labor Law* provides, 'Laborers have the right to be employed on an equal basis and choose occupations.' Article 12 further provides, 'Labourers shall not be discriminated against in employment due to their ethnic group, race, sex, or religious belief.' Article 46 says that, 'Distribution of wages shall follow the principle of distribution according to work and equal pay for equal work.' All these provisions contain the principles of equal employment and prohibit discrimination in employment. However, the *Labor Law* only specifies prohibited grounds of discrimination and does not contain detailed rules, which makes the clauses concerning discrimination difficult to enforce.

Furthermore, the *Law on Protection of Rights and Interests of Women*[23] and the *Law on Protection of Persons with Disabilities*[24] both include provisions on the employment of women and persons with disabilities, and prohibit discrimination against sex and disability. Unfortunately, although these two laws allow victims of discrimination to bring a lawsuit to the courts,[25] there is no clear administrative enforcement body to supervise employers and support victims when they are discriminated against. Thus, enforceability of the anti-discrimination rules under these two laws remains limited.

Nonetheless, a remarkable step in anti-discrimination legislation was made in China in the form of the *Employment Promotion Law*, passed in 2007 and which came into force on 1 January 2008. This law dedicates a specific chapter providing for fair employment and prohibits discrimination based on ethnic group, race, gender, or religious belief.[26] It also provides that workers from rural areas should enjoy equal rights to city residents, and discrimination against migrant workers coming from rural areas is prohibited.[27] Consequently, according to the above-mentioned laws, seven grounds of discrimination are prohibited by existing Chinese law, including discrimination based on race, ethnicity, religion, gender, disability, carrying infectious pathogens, and social origin (rural or urban).[28] More importantly, in accordance with the *Employment Promotion Law*, workers who suffer discrimination may bring a lawsuit to the people's courts,[29] and an employer who violates the law by impairing the legitimate rights and interests of workers is liable to pay compensation.[30] These provisions make it clear that discrimination victims are entitled to relief: an important step for the enforceability of the rules of anti-discrimination. Unfortunately, the *Employment Promotion Law* does not provide the employee with

[23] Adopted 3 Apr. 1992, entry into force 1 Oct. 1992, amended 28 Aug. 2005; see Chapter IV.

[24] Adopted 28 Dec. 1990, entry into force 15 May 1991, amended 28 Aug. 2008; see Chapter IV.

[25] *Law on Protection of Rights and Interests of Women*, Art. 52 (1992); *Law on Protection of Persons with Disabilities*, Art. 64 (1990).

[26] *Employment Promotion Law*, Art. 3 (2007).

[27] *Employment Promotion Law*, Art. 31 (2007).

[28] *Labor Law*, Art. 12 (1994); *Law on Protection of Persons with Disabilities*, Art. 3 (1990); *Employment Promotion Law*, Art. 30, 31 (2007).

[29] *Employment Promotion Law*, Art. 62 (2007).

[30] *Employment Promotion Law*, Art. 68 (2007).

specific remedies for discrimination suffered, nor does it provide specific liability for violation of the law.[31]

Besides legislation at the national level, regulations issued by related administrative departments also contain certain rules prohibiting discrimination. For example, in 2007 the Ministry of Labor and Social Security enacted the Provisions on Employment Services and Employment Management; one of its aims was to regulate job applications and recruitment and prohibit discrimination.[32] The provisions complement the *Employment Promotion Law* in various ways.[33] To combat discrimination in relation to the HBV, in 2007 the Ministry of Labor and Social Security issued its 'Opinions on Safeguarding the Employment Rights of Hepatitis B Carriers'. In March 2010, the Ministry of Human Resources and Social Security, the Ministry of Education and the Ministry of Health again jointly issued the 'Notice on Further Regulating Health Examination Items for Education Enrolment and Employment, Protecting the Rights of Hepatitis B Virus Carriers in Education Enrolment and Employment', which contains clear provisions about health examination and protection of HBV carriers' equal right to employment. These rules play an important role in law enforcement, which are more specific and provide clear guidance for the courts and administrative bodies to enforce the rules on anti-discrimination.

Given the above legal provisions, it is safe to say that China has established a legal framework on anti-discrimination in employment. The laws and rules contain provisions about prohibited grounds of discrimination, the enforcement body and victims' access to the courts. These legal rules provide a legal basis for administrative bodies and courts to handle discrimination cases and entitle victims to bring their claims to the administrative authorities and courts. There are several driving forces for this progress. First, the overall strategy of rule of law and establishing a harmonious society is an important background for legal development in anti-discrimination. The amendments to the Constitution in 1999 and 2004 reflect a Chinese strategy of implementing the rule of law and protecting human rights. The amendment in 1999 added an important clause providing that China implements the policy of rule of law and establishing a socialist state with a rule of law,[34] and the amendment in 2004 inserted a new clause that provides, 'the state shall respect and protect human rights'.[35] Besides China's efforts concerning the rule of law, building a harmonious society including harmonious labor relations is an important recent

[31] Crystal Roberts, Student Author, *Far from a Harmonious Society: Employment Discrimination in China*, 52 Santa Clara L. Rev. 1531 (2012), at 1552.

[32] Ministry of Labor and Social Security of the People's Republic of China, *Provisions on Employment Services and Employment Management*, Order No. 28, Arts 4, 5, 9, 16, 18, 19 and 20 (2007).

[33] Timothy Webster, *Ambivalence and Activism: Employment Discrimination in China*, 44 Vand. J. Transnat'l L. 643, 680 (2011).

[34] Constitution of The People's Republic of China, Art. 5 (1982).

[35] Ibid. at Art. 33.

goal in China.[36] Against this background, harmonious labor relations and their legal protection were placed on the agenda of the Government. During this period, several important pieces of labor legislation were adopted by the National People's Congress.[37] Hence, laws and rules concerning anti-discrimination formed part of the overall strategy of rule of law and building a harmonious society. Second, increasing awareness of equality and the impact of cases is a driving force for progress made in legislation. In recent years, people's awareness of equality has been increasing, with applicants and employees frequently bringing cases to the courts. These cases have often been reported by the media and have given rise to public attention.[38] This kind of grassroots effort is an important factor in spurring anti-discrimination legislation. Third, international covenants, especially ILO conventions and recommendations, also contribute to legal development in China. The Chinese Government ratified ILO Equal Remuneration Convention, 1951 (No. 100) in 1990 and ILO Discrimination (Employment and Occupation) Convention, 1958 (No. 111) in 2006, which are important driving forces for the development of Chinese anti-discrimination law. The principles of equality and anti-discrimination in these international instruments have been incorporated into Chinese domestic labor legislation.

It is remarkable that China has made such significant progress in employment discrimination legislation. However, this progress has been far from sufficient and much room for improvement still exists. The rules are still too general and lack detail, which will make the related law and regulations difficult to enforce. In addition, the major rules on discrimination are contained in the *Employment Promotion Law*, which prompts an important unanswered question: whether the rules of anti-discrimination cover other stages such as working terms and conditions, promotion, dismissal, and social benefits, given the *Employment Promotion Law* mainly deals with issues concerning employment at the stage of job application and recruitment. From this perspective, the insertion of rules on anti-discrimination into the *Employment Promotion Law* is problematic. Accordingly, a specific law on anti-discrimination in the workplace would help to resolve the above problems.

[36] For e.g., in 2006, an important policy document was adopted by the Central Committee of CPC in China. The document was *CPC Central Committee on the Decision on Certain Key Issues Concerning Building a Harmonious Socialist Society*. For more information on the policy document in Chinese, see Xinhua News Agency, http://cpc.people.com.cn/GB/64093/64094/4932424.html.

[37] In 2007, the *Labor Contract Law* (adopted 29 Jun. 2007, entry into force 1 Jan. 2008) and the *Labor Dispute Mediation and Arbitration Law* (adopted 29 Dec. 2007, entry into force 1 May 2008) were also passed by the National People's Congress.

[38] As anti-discrimination law is a relatively new area in China, many victims of discrimination, and supporting agencies, publicize cases to raise public awareness.

3.4 Implementation Mechanism for the Anti-discrimination Law

The importance of anti-discrimination in employment is reflected not only in the law itself, but also in its implementation. As the law on anti-discrimination in employment forms part of labor law, the mechanism for implementation should be explored within the general framework of labor law. In general, China's anti-discrimination implementation mechanism lies in administrative and judicial procedures.

3.4.1 The Administrative Implementation Mechanism

The *Labor Law* stipulates a general administrative implementation mechanism. According to Article 85 of the *Labor Law*, the labor administrative agencies of governments at or above the county level have the authority to supervise and inspect the implementation by employers of laws, rules and regulations on labor. They also have the power to terminate any acts that violate laws, rules and regulations on labor and order rectification. Under this article, labor administrative agencies should have the power to supervise and inspect discrimination committed by employers. However, the *Labor and Social Security Inspection Regulations* promulgated by the State Council in 2004 does not provide for the inspection power of labor agencies in cases of discrimination.[39] The regulation does not include a general anti-discrimination requirement, although it includes specific provisions relating to female employees.[40] Consequently, under this regulation governmental labor agencies do not have specific responsibilities to combat discrimination.

The *Employment Promotion Law* of 2007 contains new provisions compared with the *Labor and Social Security Inspection Regulations* of 2004. Chapter III of this law concerns fair employment. Article 60 of the law stipulates that the administrative agencies of labor shall supervise and inspect implementation of this law and establish a reporting system to accept reports on violations of the law, and shall verify and handle such violations in a timely manner. Accordingly, administrative labor agencies are entitled to accept and deal with employment discrimination cases.

Nevertheless, in practice, the role of labor agencies is still limited in combating discrimination. In addition to the unclear responsibility specified by law, another important reason limiting the role of labor agencies is a practical one. In China,

[39] State Council of The People's Republic of China, *Regulation on Labor and Social Security Inspection Regulations*, No. 423, Art. 11 (2004).

[40] Ronald C. Brown, *China's Employment Discrimination Law During Economic Transition*, 19 Colum. J. Asian L. 361, 415 (2006). See also State Council of The People's Republic of China, ibid. at Art. 11 (2004).

labor agencies have broad jurisdiction over employment matters, including wages, social insurance, working hours, labor contracts, dismissal, working safety, and so on. Their large caseloads to some extent prevent them from becoming deeply involved in discrimination cases. According to the statistics, in 2011, labor agencies inspected 1,848,000 employers on the spot, inspected 2,108,000 employers by reviewing their submitted written documents, and handled 380,000 cases of labor violations. However, in 2011 only about 25,000 full-time inspectors were working in labor agencies.[41] Such huge caseloads and few personnel make it difficult for labor agencies to actively deal with discrimination cases. For labor agencies in China, more serious cases directly infringing employee's interests in relation to wages and social insurance have been considered more important and urgent. For example, from 2011, labor agencies have required employers to pay salaries totalling Chinese Yuan Renminbi (CNY, Yuan) 15.51 billion to workers and have required 128,000 employers to pay a social insurance fee of CNY 5.28 billion for workers.[42] Accordingly, in reality, few discrimination cases are handled by the labor agencies.

3.4.2 Labor Arbitration and Litigation Proceedings

In China, labor arbitration is mandatory when labor disputes arise.[43] If the persons concerned are not satisfied with the results of the arbitration, they can bring the case to a court.[44] Whether a case is a 'labor dispute' or not is a key element for the remedy procedure. Although the *Labor Dispute Mediation and Arbitration Law* of 2007 lists several types of labor dispute which are applicable to the labor mediation and arbitration procedure, employment discrimination is not regarded as one of them.[45] Consequently, arbitration commissions usually do not accept employment discrimination cases. In addition, the *Employment Promotion Law* stipulates that, for any discrimination in employment in violation of its provisions, the workers concerned may bring a lawsuit to the courts.[46] However, this law does not explicitly stipulate that workers who suffer discrimination in employment can bring their cases to arbitration commissions. Thus, currently in China, employment discrimination cases are often adjudicated, which is different from the procedure applicable to other

[41] See Ministry of Human Resources and Social Security of the People's Republic of China, *Bulletin of Statistics for the Development of Human Resources and Social Security in China of 2011*.

[42] Ibid.

[43] In China, according to the *Labor Law* and *Labor Dispute Mediation and Arbitration Law*, all labor cases should be brought to arbitration commissions first and if the parties are dissatisfied with the arbitration, they can appeal the cases to courts.

[44] *Labor Dispute Mediation and Arbitration Law*, Art. 5 (2007).

[45] Ibid. at Art. 2 (2007).

[46] *Employment Promotion Law*, Art. 68 (2007).

labor cases for which arbitrations are required before being brought to the courts. The major reason for the difference is that discrimination cases are very new in China compared with other traditional labor cases. Specifically, the legislature seems to have more confidence in the capacity of the courts in handling discrimination cases than the administrative agencies and the labor arbitration commissions in the background, where the discrimination law is still general and weak with no specific administrative agency responsible for employment discrimination.[47] However, whether the difference is reasonable or not is worth reconsidering.[48]

3.4.3 Typical Discrimination Cases

Since coming into effect on 1 January 2008, the *Employment Promotion Law* has generated a large number of lawsuits challenging a few types of employment discrimination.[49] The following are some well-known cases on employment discrimination which reflect the attitude and capacity of courts in China in dealing with discrimination cases recently.

3.4.3.1 Sex Discrimination

The first typical case is *Cao v. Juren Education Group* (2012). This is probably the first publicly reported case of gender discrimination in employment among university students since the *Employment Promotion Law* came into force in 2008.[50] In June 2012, Cao submitted her resume to Juren to apply for an administrative assistant position, but was rejected by Juren because of the 'male only' requirement. Cao brought a lawsuit in the court. The court has not yet come to a final decision. However, Juren already changed its employment advertisement and the gender requirement disappeared. In many jurisdictions, 'male only' is often regarded as obvious sex discrimination, except if the employer has good cause. However, some employers in China still often impose a sex requirement in job advertisements.

[47] *An Interpretation of the Employment Promotion Law in the PRC* 179 (Chunying Xin ed., Law Press 2007).

[48] In China, debate is lively and ongoing on the labor dispute resolution system. Some argue that the compulsory arbitration procedure and the court procedure are long and time-consuming and that mandatory arbitration should be abolished. In the view of the author, the arbitration system has its historical background and this procedure will greatly reduce the cases brought to courts. The difference in the dispute resolution system between discrimination cases and other labor cases is another issue and needs to be discussed further.

[49] Timothy Webster, *Ambivalence and Activism: Employment Discrimination in China*, 44 Vand. J. Transnat'l L. 643 (2011), at 692.

[50] See Lu Lin, *Sex Discrimination in Employment Rights' Cases Takes a Big Step*, People's Daily Online, 9 Aug. 2012 (available in Chinese at http://edu.people.com.cn/n/2012/0809/c1053-18704935.html) (accessed 1 Aug. 2013).

According to a survey, about 21 % of job posts have a sex requirement.[51] Many employers do not intend to discriminate, but their lack of awareness of sex equality often puts persons of a certain sex in a disadvantaged situation. The court's slow action in this case also shows that the court's capacity in handling discrimination cases needs to be improved.

The second typical sex discrimination case is a retirement age case. *Zhou v. The Pingdingshan Branch of China's Construction Bank* (2005, 2006)[52] is about female employees' compulsory retirement at the age of 55. It is probably the first reported case in judicial proceedings to challenge the constitutionality of the retirement age of female workers. Zhou, a 55-year-old woman, was an employee of the Bank. In January 2005, she was informed that she was at the age of retirement and the Bank had already started the process for her retirement. Zhou thought that it is discriminatory that female and male workers retire at different ages (for female, 55; for male, 60). She then applied for arbitration in the local arbitration commission, where she lost. In October, Zhou brought the case to court. The court affirmed that the employer's decisions were consistent with national policies and legislation regarding the retirement age and rejected the plaintiff's claim. This is an important case on discrimination and the age of retirement. Under Chinese law and regulation, there are different retirement ages for men and women.[53] It is notable that for a long time and even now, many countries have different retirement ages for both sexes. These differences are acceptable by law in many countries including some European countries. Although Zhou failed in the case, the fact that the court agreed to hear the case at all is of itself worthy of recognition. It demonstrates that awareness of equality for workers is increasing and the courts are sometimes positive in handling cases.

Another typical sex discrimination case concerns pregnancy. This is *Furende Hongshanhu Jewelry International (Beijing) CO. LTD. v. Mrs. Jin* (2011).[54] Jin was an employee of Furende. In 2009, the company adjusted her post due to her pregnancy, which was rejected by Jin. In 2010, she was fired. She then filed a case with labor arbitration claiming restitution. The arbitration commission supported the claim by the employee. The court also affirmed the decision of the arbitration commission. In China, victims of pregnancy discrimination can easily obtain a remedy. Whether pregnancy discrimination is sex discrimination is unclear, but the *Labor Law* and *Labor Contract Law* expressly prohibit employers from dismissing pregnant workers, except for misconduct.[55] Consequently, dismissing a pregnant worker without misconduct will constitute unfair dismissal and the dismissed worker can

[51] Dingjian Cai, *Employment Discrimination in China: Current Conditions and Anti-discrimination Strategies*, China Social Science Press, 2007, p. 513.

[52] 2005, Labor Dispute Arbitration Committee of Pingdingshan City, No. 86; 2006 Zhan, Civil, First, No. 31.

[53] For more information about the retirement age, see State Council of the PRC, *Interim Provisions on Retirement and Resignation of Workers Rectified by the Standing Committee of the National People's Congress* (3 Jun. 1978).

[54] 2011, Chaoyang District, Civil, First, No. 04594.

[55] *Labor Law*, Art. 29 (1994); *Labor Contract Law*, Art. 42 (2007).

easily obtain a remedy under the dismissal law. Consequently, in China, the plaintiffs in such cases can easily win because of express provisions in labor laws instead of laws or regulations on discrimination.

3.4.3.2 Health Discrimination

A typical case is on the HBV: *Guo v. Foxconn (Hangzhou) Co. Ltd* (2007).[56] In May 2007, Guo applied for a job as Information Commissioner with Foxconn Co. Ltd., and passed both a written test and an interview. But in June he was informed he was not to be admitted because he was an HBV carrier. In September 2007, Guo filed a lawsuit, claiming compensation for mental suffering. Finally, both parties reached a settlement under the intermediation of the court. In China recently, there have been more and more HBV cases. As a response to this case and other HBV cases, in 2007 and 2010 the relevant authorities issued two legal documents[57] concerning medical examinations to protect HBV carriers from being discriminated against. The 2010 document prohibits employers and schools from requesting HBV testing in medical examinations, requesting the results of an applicant's HBV tests, or asking the applicant if they carry the antigen. Medical institutions are likewise banned from giving schools or employers the results of a medical examination.[58] The document also recognizes the privacy rights of applicants and further includes sanctions against employers and schools that illegally request HBV examinations.[59] In recent years, plaintiffs in HBV cases have often won their cases mainly because these two documents expressly prohibit discrimination against HBV carriers. Such legal documents are very helpful in rooting out HBV discrimination.

A typical case on HIV is *Wu v. Education Bureau and Human Resources and Social Security Bureau in Anqing City* (2011).[60] In May 2010, Wu took an examination for a teaching position, organized by the Education Bureau and the Human Resources and Social Security Bureau in Anqing City, and passed the test and interview. In August, Wu's application was rejected because he was an HIV carrier. In August 2010, Wu brought a suit to court, but the court dismissed his claim. So far,

[56] 2009, Hangjiang, Civil, First, No. 1981.

[57] In May 2007, the Ministry of Labor and Social Security issued its *Opinion on Safeguarding the Employment Rights of Hepatitis B Virus Carriers*. In February 2010, the Ministry of Human Resources and Social Security, the Ministry of Education and the Ministry of Health jointly issued the *Notice on Further Regulating Health Examination Items for Education Enrolment and Employment, Protecting the Rights of Hepatitis B Virus Carriers in Education Enrolment and Employment*.

[58] Timothy Webster, *Ambivalence and Activism: Employment Discrimination in China*, 44 Vand. J. Transnat'l L. 643 (2011), at 681.

[59] Ministry of Human Resource and Social Security, the Ministry of Education and the Ministry of Health of the PRC, *Notice on Further Regulating Health Examination Items for Education Enrolment and Employment, Protecting the Rights of Hepatitis B Virus Carriers in Education Enrolment and Employment* (2010).

[60] 2011, Yi, Administrative, Final, No. 0022.

there have not been many HIV cases in China, partly because there are no detailed rules prohibiting HIV discrimination similar to HBV. There is only a general article in the Regulation of HIV Prevention and Treatment of 2006, which stipulates that no entity or individual should discriminate against HIV carriers, patients and their family members, whose lawful rights and interest in marriage, employment and education should be protected.[61] The provisions in this regulation are far from sufficient. Due to the fact that HIV might be infectious in some ways and people often have concerns about contact with HIV carriers, sometimes it is difficult for the court to balance the justification of employers against the equal treatment of applicants and employees. In China, this is a very new issue and it takes time to improve legislation and enforcement.

Another type of health discrimination is gene discrimination. A typical case is *Tang, Zhou, Xie v. Human Resources and Social Security Bureau in Foshan City* (2009).[62] This is probably the first reported case of genetic discrimination in China. Xie applied for a civil service position and passed the test and interview. But he failed to get access to the follow-up recruitment process because he was considered unqualified in the health examination where he was identified as a patient with haemopathy, carrying thalassaemia. In 2009, Xie filed a lawsuit, claiming it was illegal that the defendant did not hire him because of his health examination result. Xie lost the case. However, it was notable that during the final judgment the court gave judicial advice to the relevant authority, suggesting that it conduct a study on whether patients with thalassaemia who have no obvious clinical symptoms should be disqualified from being civil servants. As having certain genes is not a legally prohibited ground of discrimination, the court could do nothing. But the court's advice sent to the authority is very meaningful. It implies that even where the court cannot adjudicate in favour of the plaintiff it will show its concern for potential indications of discrimination.

3.4.3.3 Disability Discrimination

A typical case is *Xuan v. Human Resources and Social Security Bureau in Anhui Province* (2011).[63] This is probably the first case of disability discrimination for civil servants. Xuan took the 2012 National Civil Service Examination after graduation in June 2011. He brought a lawsuit to court in December 2011, claiming that it was illegal that the defendant did not provide accessibility services for the examination and restricted blind people from taking the civil service examination. The court ruled that the defendant's act was legal. This case brought up some important

[61] State Council of the PRC, *Regulation on HIV Prevention and Treatment*, No. 457, Art. 3 (29 Jan. 2006).

[62] 2010, Foshan, Intermediate, Administrative, Final, No. 381.

[63] See Xinhuanet.com, *The Trial of the First Case of Disability Discrimination in Civil Servant Exam Begins and Application of Law Becomes the Focus*, 7 Jun. 2012 (available in Chinese at http://news.xinhuanet.com/legal/2012-06/07/c_123246340.htm) (accessed 2 Aug. 2013).

legal issues about disability discrimination. First, the *Law on the Protection of Persons with Disabilities* does require employers to provide 'reasonable accommodation' for employees,[64] but how to define 'reasonable' remains unanswered, and will continue to be a problem in the future. More practically, the law only states that, 'employers should provide reasonable accommodation to its employees…'.[65] But whether employers have the same duty to offer it during the job application and recruitment stages needs to be clarified. That was a key issue in this case. It is laudable to specify the employers' duty of reasonable accommodation in the law, but how to interpret and apply this rule is unresolved.

3.4.3.4 Height Discrimination

A typical height discrimination case is *Jiang v. Chengdu's Branch of People's Bank of China* (2001).[66] This is probably the first publicly reported case of height discrimination in China. Jiang, a law student at university, applied for a position in the Bank but was rejected because his height did not satisfy the bank requirement that male and female applicants be over 168 cm and 155 cm respectively. Jiang sued the bank in the court in December 2001. In January 2002, the Bank revised its employment advertisement and deleted the height requirement. But the court dismissed the case, holding that it was out of the scope of cases stipulated by the *Administrative Litigation Law*.[67] This case was interesting and raised an important issue. In many countries, height or physical appearance is not a legally prohibited ground of discrimination. If someone is discriminated against because of their height or physical appearance, whether and how to provide a legal remedy remains unanswered in China and some other countries.

3.4.3.5 Age Discrimination

A typical case is *Yang v. Ministry of Personnel* (2005).[68] Yang, 36 years old, was an LLM student. Before he registered for the civil service examination, he found out that the job advertisement required candidates to be less than 35 years old. So, Yang brought a lawsuit to the court. The court refused to accept the case because the court believed the case was beyond the scope of administrative litigation. Then Yang appealed to a higher court, but the court dismissed the appeal and delivered the same judgment as the original one.

---

[64] *Law on the Protection of Persons with Disabilities*, Art. 38 (1990).

[65] Ibid. at Art. 38.

[66] 2002 Wuhouhang, First, No. 3.

[67] As the defendant in this case was a branch of the People's Bank of China, which is the central bank, the *Administrative Litigation Law* (1989) was applied in the case.

[68] 2005, Second Intermediate, Administrative, First, No. 578.

Age so far is not a prohibited ground of discrimination in China, so it is difficult for persons discriminated against to win cases. In China, because of the lack of related rules and age equality awareness, many employers impose an age requirement in their job advertisements, many of which are unreasonable. But before age is added to the field of prohibited discrimination, the court can do nothing. Even so, given that the age requirement in many job postings is unreasonable and discriminatory, government bodies and employers should voluntarily review their policies and job postings on the age requirement to prevent discrimination. More importantly, rules on age discrimination should be put on the national legislation agenda.

3.4.3.6 Implications of Typical Cases

The cases above generally indicate that anti-discrimination in China is now not only an issue in law or in theory, but an important practical one. This is a positive trend. From the above cases, some points can be inferred.

First, in general not many employment discrimination cases are brought to arbitration commissions or courts in China and the role of judicial organs is still limited at present. Despite the role litigation has played so far in unleashing enthusiasm about the anti-discrimination movement, litigating employment discrimination is still an unpopular proposition in China.[69] A survey shows that the number of employment discrimination cases from the courts presents an extremely small percentage of the overall number of cases.[70] This is partly because of the position of the courts. Chinese courts have some discretion in deciding whether to accept discrimination cases. Some courts refuse to accept cases of discrimination in hiring because it is not clearly listed in the Supreme People's Court's causes of action.[71] The causes of action issued by the Supreme Court do not expressly include employment discrimination.[72]

Two other reasons might contribute to the small number of cases. One is the difficulty of the burden proof for employees; the other is a weak awareness of rights by employees. As to the burden of proof, plaintiffs must satisfy a heavy burden of proof in employment discrimination claims. In some countries, such as the US, once the plaintiff has established a prima facie case of discrimination, the burden of proof shifts to the defendant to provide a non-discriminatory reason for its decision. In

[69] Jiefeng Lu, *Curb Your Enthusiasm: A Note on Employment Discrimination Lawsuits in China*, 10 Rich. J. Global L. & Bus. 211, 214 (2010–2011).

[70] Ibid. at 220–221.

[71] Timothy Webster, *Ambivalence and Activism: Employment Discrimination in China*, 44 Vand. J. Transnat'l L. 643 (2011), at 697.

[72] See Supreme People's Court of the PRC, *The Provisions on the Causes of Action of Civil Cases* (issued in 2007 and revised in 2011).

contrast, Chinese laws do not articulate an evidentiary standard and do not include the same burden-shifting between plaintiffs and defendants.[73]

In addition, as anti-discrimination law is very new in China, many persons discriminated against just keep silent due to weak awareness or some other practical issue, such as the cost of litigation. A survey shows that many persons discriminated against do not have the incentive to bring cases to the courts because of the cost of litigation and lack of confidence in the courts. Instead of seeking relief from the courts, employees might keep silent or choose other ways, such as asking for help from the media or filing complaints with the competent authority.[74] Although laws, especially the *Employment Promotion Law*, provide a possibility for the victim to seek relief, it is still difficult to win cases in judicial procedures. Judgments indicate that the courts are relatively conservative and interpret laws carefully and discreetly. Due to a lack of detailed rules and experience of dealing with discrimination cases, the courts' capacity in handling cases remains weak.[75]

Second, despite the foregoing, awareness of equality by the courts, employers and the public is improving. First, public awareness of equality has been strengthened, and the law and the public cannot tolerate obvious discrimination such as HVB discrimination; second, the courts are more active than before. More courts are willing to accept discrimination cases and are more positive in handling discrimination cases. During 2000–2011, the number of famous cases has increased dramatically mainly because of the adoption of the *Employment Promotion Law* and the *Labor Contract Law*.[76] Among those cases in 2000–2011, more than half the plaintiffs won their cases or received positive support from the courts.[77] Some courts even ordered defendants to pay damages for mental suffering to plaintiffs who suffered discrimination.[78] In some cases, the courts sent judicial advice to the defendant, including governmental organs, on matters such as standards of health examination. Moreover, although some plaintiffs lost their cases, employers often corrected their discriminatory acts, for example, modifying their recruitment advertisements before the courts make decisions.

---

[73] Crystal Roberts, Student Author, *Far from a Harmonious Society: Employment Discrimination in China*, 52 Santa Clara L. Rev. 1531 (2012), at 1555.

[74] Shijian Yang, *The Ways and Reasons of Courts in Handling Employment Discrimination Cases*, in "*Theory and Practice of Antidiscrimination in the Workplace*" 100–101 (Xiaonan Liu ed., Law Press 2012).

[75] So far, there are no accurate numbers of caseloads handled by the courts.

[76] Wei Zhou, *From Height to Gene: The Legal Development of Chinese Antidiscrimination* in "*Theory and Practice of Antidiscrimination in the Workplace*" (Xiaonan Liu ed., Law Press 2012), p. 18.

[77] Ibid. at 19–20.

[78] In a health discrimination case in 2008 handled by the Chaoyang District Court in Beijing, the court ordered the defendant to make an apology to the plaintiff and pay compensation of CNY 17,000 for economic loss, and CNY 2000 for mental suffering: Wei Zhou, *From Height to Gene: The Legal Development of Chinese Antidiscrimination* in "*Theory and Practice of Antidiscrimination in the Workplace*" (Xiaonan Liu ed., Law Press 2012), p. 23.

Third, the government is more active in anti-discrimination. The rules and regulations mentioned above demonstrate that public attention and opinion can put pressure on the government into taking relevant measures. Although the legal base is not very strong, the government has begun to recognize its legal obligation to combat discrimination and protect the equality of job applicants and employees. Labor agencies[79] at the local level often accept cases of obvious employment discrimination and rectify misconduct by employers, although such cases are still few.

Fourth, the media play an important role in anti-discrimination by publicizing cases, exerting pressure on employers and raising public awareness of equality in employment. The media are relatively active in reporting discrimination cases. A survey conducted shows that in 2008–2011 there were 284 reports in ten key print newspapers including the *People's Daily*, the *Legal Daily*, and so on. The forms of report include general comments, reports on people, news updates§ and policy advocacy and the topics reported covered different types of discrimination, such as disability, *Hu Kou*, health, age, social origin, physical appearance, sex, political affiliation and others.[80] Most of the cases introduced above were reported by the media and the public pays much attention to the result of cases, which is helpful in pushing the courts to be more active and apply the law more professionally. Winning in most cases is partly due to media reports and pressure of public opinion.[81]

Lastly, the role of non-governmental organizations (NGOs) in anti-discrimination in employment is increasingly important. Some NGOs assist victims through lawsuits, which is not only conducive to safeguarding the rights of victims but also helps to increase public and employer awareness of anti-discrimination and equality, often with the help of the media. In addition, through academic research and, for example, putting forward legal proposals,[82] NGOs promote improvements to legislation as well as lobbying the government for implementation of anti-discrimination law.[83] Some argue that Chinese citizens, with the assistance of civil society groups

[79] Under the *Labor Law* of 1994, labor agencies have broad power to inspect and correct employers' misconduct concerning workplace rules, working time, wages, work safety, child labor, unfair dismissal, etc. As mentioned at section §9.04[A] above, under the *Employment Promotion Law* (2007), labor agencies also have jurisdiction over employment discrimination.

[80] Xiaonan Liu, Liwan Wang, *Survey Analysis on the Reports on Antidiscrimination in the Workplace Conducted by the Chinese Key Print Media in 2008–2011* in "*Theory and Practice of Antidiscrimination in the Workplace*" (Xiaonan Liu ed., Law Press 2012), pp. 67–73.

[81] Wei Zhou, *From Height to Gene: The Legal Development of Chinese Antidiscrimination* in "*Theory and Practice of Antidiscrimination in the Workplace*" (Xiaonan Liu ed., Law Press 2012), p. 25.

[82] NGOs active in policy advocacy, for example the Institute of Constitutionalism in the Chinese University of Policy Science and Law, published The Suggested Version of an Anti-employment-discrimination Law in 2010: see *The Suggested Version of an Anti-employment-discrimination Law and Overseas Experience* (Dingjian Cai & Xiaonan Liu eds., Social Sciences Academic Press China 2010).

[83] In recent years, some NGOs have been actively involved in anti-discrimination by providing legal aid to victims, researching and advising the government. These NGOs include, for example, the Institute of Constitutionalism at the China University of Political Science and Law, the Centre of Human Rights of Sichuan University, and the Yirenping Organization in Beijing.

and online technologies, can effectuate legal change in a gradual, small-scale way.[84] Indeed, the role of NGOs and the media, particularly the internet, is actually more and more important in Chinese society.

3.5 Future Challenges and Tasks in Anti-discrimination in Employment

3.5.1 Improving Legislation on Anti-discrimination in Employment

Given the foregoing analysis, it is safe to say that China has established a basic legal frame work for anti-discrimination in employment. However, the related rules are still in rough draft. Some provisions, such as the responsibility of administrative agencies, definition of discrimination, grounds of prohibited discrimination, burden of proof, as well as relief available to victims, are unclear or insufficient.

It is notable that age discrimination is not prohibited in China's legislation. So, literally speaking, an employer can, at will, set an age restriction as a mandatory qualification for employment. This makes age discrimination and age classification common forms of employment discrimination in China.[85] In the labor market, it is difficult to find a job advertisement with no age limit. As China is gradually moving towards an aging society, it is of great theoretical and practical significance to prohibit age discrimination.[86] In addition, much discrimination is based on appearance, height, genes, and so on, which are also not expressly prohibited by international covenants. How to resolve such discrimination needs to be put on the agenda of the legislature.

Furthermore, clarifying the definition of discrimination is an urgent matter. Without a clear definition of discrimination, the courts will find it difficult to make judgments. In addition, despite the right to bring lawsuits in Chinese courts for employment discrimination, the *Employment Promotion Law* does not provide the employee with specific remedies for discrimination suffered, nor does it provide any specific liability for violation of the law.[87] Finally, besides the recruitment

---

[84] Timothy Webster, *Ambivalence and Activism: Employment Discrimination in China*, 44 Vand. J. Transnat'l L. 643 (2011), at 705.

[85] See Wei Zhou, *On the Age Discrimination in Employment of Our Country: An Empirical Study of 300,000 Advertisements for Employees in Shanghai and Chengdu from 1995 to 2005*, 3 J. Pol. Sci. & L. Forum 13, 13 21 (2007) referenced in Jiefeng Lu, *Employment Discrimination in China: The Current Situation and Principle Challenges*, 32 Hamline L. Rev. 133 (2009), at 154.

[86] Sichuan University School of Law, *Chinese Courts and Arbitration Bodies Prohibiting Employment Discrimination Case Selection* (International Labor Organization Beijing 2011) (in Chinese).

[87] Na Lan, *Is There New Hope in Labor Rights Protection for Chinese Migrant Workers?*, 10 Asian-Pac. L. & Pol'y J. 482, 483 (2009) referenced in Crystal Roberts, Student Author, *Far from a Harmonious Society: Employment Discrimination in China*, 52 Santa Clara L. Rev. 1531 (2012), at 1552.

process, statutory clarification is required as to whether discrimination laws and rules cover other stages and aspects of employment including working conditions, wages, promotion, training, social benefits and dismissal. Consequently, China's legislators should pass a law specifically addressing discrimination in employment in order to provide clear rules against employment discrimination.[88]

3.5.2 Strengthening Education on Awareness and Attitude of Employers

The battle against discrimination takes place in many forums but perhaps none are as important as education. Citizens must be provided information to combat the exclusionary stereotypes that women are inferior to men, that age determines ability, and that race and ethnicity determine competence.[89] In addition, one of the main challenges facing China is the long-term education of the population regarding the fallacies of discrimination as well as its costs and dangers to society.[90] Education is an important part of preventing discrimination. As mentioned above, a large number of discriminatory acts are not intentional but unconscious because of a weak sense of law and equality, as well as an incorrect understanding on employment issues. For example, HBV discrimination often results from the employer's lack of knowledge of HBV. Therefore, government agencies as well as social organizations should strengthen education for employers and the public to eliminate the incorrect understanding and even prejudice of employers and society as a whole. Only when employers have a correct understanding of employment issues and sufficient legal awareness can discrimination be effectively prevented and reduced. This is particularly important. Additionally, employers should change their thinking in relation to the job market. Before the reform and opening-up policy, China implemented a planned economy system, labor was allocated by the state, and employers had no choice. Since the policy of reform and opening-up, employers have been given the freedom to choose their employees. In this transition, the freedom of employers is often over-emphasized. So, through the law, the government should change employers' ideas and help them to realize that the freedom of employers should be subject to the law and should not discriminate against applicants and employees in the workplace.[91]

---

[88] Crystal Roberts, Student Author, *Far from a Harmonious Society: Employment Discrimination in China*, 52 Santa Clara L. Rev. 1531 (2012), at 1558.

[89] Ronald C. Brown, *China's Employment Discrimination Law During Economic Transition*, 19 Colum. J. Asian L. 361 (2006), at 419.

[90] Ronald C. Brown, *China's Employment Discrimination Law During Economic Transition*, 19 Colum. J. Asian L. 361 (2006), at 420.

[91] In the transition period to a market economy, due to the short history of anti-discrimination, many employers including some government officials often believe that employers enjoy complete freedom in employment matters without limitation.

3.5.3 Improving the Role of Government in Anti-discrimination in Employment

In terms of the provisions of international conventions and national laws, the principles of anti-discrimination in the employment and legislative frameworks in different jurisdictions are basically similar. But law enforcement, especially the role of administrative agencies in anti-discrimination, differs considerably. While employees can seek relief through private action by filing cases with an arbitration commission or the courts, this is limited because of the high cost of private actions.[92]

Many countries attach great importance to the role of administrative agencies. For example, the US and other countries have established an administrative body for anti-discrimination and the promotion of equality. The US Civil Rights Act of 1964 established the Equal Employment Opportunity Commission.[93] In addition to facilitating litigation, the EU is attempting to introduce other mechanisms. For example, The Racial Treatment Directive (2000) and the Directive on Equal Treatment, modified in 2002, require Member States to establish an independent body to promote equal treatment.[94] By comparison, the role of China's labor agencies in anti-discrimination is relatively weak, which leads to the fact that enforcement of anti-discrimination law mainly relies on private actions. Practice has proved that the role of administrative agencies in anti-discrimination is effective. For example, HBV discrimination in China had been serious for quite a long time and issuing legal documents to regulate heath examinations arranged by hospitals and employers has effectively prevented discrimination. Unfortunately, unlike the US or other countries, China does not have an Equal Employment Opportunity Commission to investigate allegations of employment discrimination.[95]

At present, it seems difficult to establish a totally independent body for anti-discrimination in China.[96] But it is advisable and feasible to establish additional bodies within the administrative labor agencies at different levels to be responsible for monitoring discrimination and promoting equality in employment. These bodies should have functions including accepting complaints from the public, educating employers and the public, issuing legally binding regulations or rules and other guidelines for employers, arbitration commissions, and the courts.

---

[92] Particularly in China, many migrant workers come from rural areas, and once disputes occur it is difficult for them to go through all the judicial procedures and live in the cities where living is much more expensive than rural areas.

[93] Civil Rights Act of 1964, Pub. L. 88–352, Title VII, section 705.

[94] Directive 2000/43/EC, at Art. 13; and Directive 2002/73/EC of the European Parliament and of the Council amending Council Directive 76/207/EEC on the implementation of the principle of equal treatment for men and women as regards access to employment, vocational training and promotion, and working conditions (23 Sep. 2002), OJ L 269, 05/10/2002 pp. 15–20, Art. 8a.

[95] Timothy Webster, *Ambivalence and Activism: Employment Discrimination in China*, 44 Vand. J. Transnat'l L. 643 (2011), at 663–664.

[96] In China, establishing a new independent body at the central level is very difficult in the context of streamlining government organs in the new century.

3.5.4 *Improving the Capability of Arbitration Commissions and the Courts*

Implementation of the law is as important as the law itself. Although Chinese laws on anti-discrimination in employment are still general, the basic legislative framework has been established and the principles of anti-discrimination and equality have been adopted. However, currently many courts are still very cautious about accepting discrimination cases. On the one hand, the courts have a huge caseload[97]; they do not like to take more cases. On the other hand, the law does not provide detailed rules, which leads the courts to become inactive in accepting cases. Although laws and regulations are general, arbitration commissions and courts should both make full use of the provisions of laws and regulations to create interpretative and technical rules so as to implement related laws and rules. For the time being, employment discrimination should be added as a cause of action in civil cases to ensure the lower courts accept employment cases. Additionally, specific judicial interpretation on employment discrimination is required so as to guide local courts in handling cases.[98]

3.6 Summary

Employment discrimination has received more attention from the public and the government in recent years. The government has taken steps towards alleviating this problem by enacting nationwide legislation. Besides efforts by the government, all players in anti-discrimination law are more active, including the administrative agencies, courts and NGOs. However, discrimination legislation is still general and the roles of administrative agencies and courts need to be enhanced. To better combat discrimination and promote equality in the workplace requires stronger legislation and detailed rules. Labor agencies and courts should be more positive in accepting cases and increasing their capacity in case handling. Anti-discrimination is a relatively new legal issue in China so that, although China has taken important steps down the right path to prohibiting discrimination, it will take time to effectively promote and protect equality in the workplace by improving legislation and law enforcement.

[97] For e.g., in 2011 courts at different levels in China accepted 6,614,049 first instance civil cases. This number does not include second instance civil cases and criminal and administrative cases. See Supreme People's Court of the PRC, http://www.court.gov.cn/qwfb/sfsj/index_1.html (accessed 7 Feb. 2013).

[98] Since adoption of the *Labor Law* in 1994, the Supreme Court has issued four specific opinions on the interpretation of certain rules applicable to labor cases (2001, 2006, 2010 and 2013). None of these covers the issue of discrimination. Actually, such interpretations play in important role in handling cases. Accordingly, it would be very helpful if the Supreme Court could issue a document interpreting the related rules concerning discrimination.

Chapter 4
Combating Employment Discrimination Against the Disabled and the Quota System

Combating discrimination against the disabled is an integral part of protection for the disabled and also an important element of labor law. Combating disability discrimination in employment has special significance for safeguarding the equal rights of and promoting employment for the disabled. It can help them become more independent and confident, to enhance their social status, and to empower them to be self-reliant. It also has an indispensible role in reducing their dependency on the government, the society, and their family. Along with the advance of technology and medical care and improvements in the work environment, the ability of many disabled to work has been enhanced and more job positions suitable for the disabled have become available. Therefore, preventing and combating disability discrimination in employment is now more important than ever. Yet compared to other forms of discrimination in employment, it is more recalcitrant. In many situations, the ability of the disabled to work is limited compared to the rest of the population and it is not easy to decide whether a person is qualified for a particular job. At the same time, having the disabled on one's staff often requires the employer to provide special equipment or facilities to meet their special needs, which might increase labor costs. Therefore, disability discrimination legislation and its implementation need to balance the equal rights to employment of the disabled and the burden and labor costs of the employer. This is much less of an issue in efforts to combat discrimination based on gender, race or other factors. In reality, this also makes it more difficult in disability discrimination cases to determine the justifications of the employer's defense.

By the end of 2010, people with disabilities totaled 85.02 million in China. Among these, 12.63 million have vision disabilities, 20.54 million hearing disabilities, 1.3 million speech disabilities, 24.72 million physical disabilities, 5.68 million intellectual disabilities, 6.29 million mental disabilities, 13.86 million multiple

Z. Xie, *Labor Law in China*, Research Series on the Chinese Dream and China's Development Path, DOI 10.1007/978-3-662-46929-3_4

disabilities. In terms of the seriousness of disability, there were 25.18 million persons with serious disability and 59.84 million persons with moderate and mild disability.[1] This shows there is a huge population of the disabled in China, and it is more important than ever to combat disability discrimination and promote employment for the disabled.

4.1 Legal Prohibition Against Disability Discrimination in Employment

Both the *Law on Protection of Persons with Disabilities* and the *Law on Employment Promotion* stipulate that employers cannot discriminate against the disabled. The *Law on Employment Promotion* states that when recruiting, the employer cannot discriminate against candidates with disabilities.[2] And according to this provision, the victim of such discrimination can bring a lawsuit in court for civil damages. But since this law does not define what constitutes "discrimination," it is hard to determine when a person with a disability has been a victim of discrimination.

The *Law on Protection of Persons with Disabilities* also has anti-discrimination provisions. It stipulates that a person with a disability cannot be discriminated against in terms of employment recruitment, promotion, professional title, labor remuneration, benefits, rest, vacation and holiday leave, and social insurance.[3] The provision is comprehensive and prohibits discrimination against the disabled in any aspect of the process of employment. In addition, this law also requires that when a disabled person's legitimate rights are violated the person has the right to request that the relevant agency handles the case, to bring the case to an arbitration agency for arbitration, or to sue in the People's Court.[4]

Provisions in these two laws that prohibit discrimination indicate that, currently in China, there is still no clear definition of "disability discrimination" in employment. Since the ability of the disabled to work is limited in many situations, the employer must make certain adjustments and accommodations in the workplace or job duties for the disabled. If there are no criteria for determining whether a person with a disability can perform the duties of a job, and no regulations concerning the employer's duty to make "reasonable accommodation," it will be very difficult to determine whether the behavior of an employer is discriminatory.

---

[1] China Disabled Persons' Federation (CDPF): *The National Total of Disabled Persons and Their Classification*, CDPF website: http://www.cdpf.org.cn/sytj/content/2012-06/26/content_30399867.htm.

[2] *The Law on Employment Promotion,* Article 29.

[3] *The Law on Protection of Persons with Disabilities,* Article 38.

[4] *The Law on Protection of Persons with Disabilities,* Article 60.

4.2 The Quota System

4.2.1 Laws and Regulations for the Quota System

According to the *Law on Protection of Persons with Disabilities*, a combination of administrative and market-based approaches should be used in employment for the disabled. Preferential policies, and supportive and protective measures need to be adopted to gradually realize broad coverage, stability, and appropriateness of employment of the disabled. The government and public institutions should run welfare enterprises which mainly hire the disabled.[5] In reality, designating a certain number of organizations to support a large presence of the disabled in their workforce has proven effective for promoting the employment of the disabled. In 2013, 369,000 more persons with disabilities get jobs in the cities, and 107,000 of them were placed in these kinds of organizations.[6]

In addition to this job creation method for the disabled, the government introduced a quota system. The employment quota system for the disabled is stipulated in the *Law on Protection of Persons with Disabilities*. It states that the government shall allot employment opportunities for the disabled in a proportionate way. All government agencies, public institutions, enterprises, and non-profit organizations shall provide employment opportunities for the disabled according to a ratio requirement and then design suitable job positions for them.[7] The *Employment Regulations for the Disabled (2007)* further specifies that the job quota for the disabled must not be lower than 1.5 % of the aggregate size of the staff. Provincial governments can set their own quota requirements in light of local conditions.[8] When an employer fails to reach the local quota requirement, they must make monetary contributions to the Fund for the Employment of the Disabled (the "*Fund*").[9]

In light of the above law and regulation, the types of employers to whom the quota requirement is applicable cover a wide range. They include all government agencies, public institutions, enterprises, and non-profit organizations. The quota system has played a positive role in promoting employment for the disabled. For example, as mentioned above, 2013 saw 369,000 new jobs created for the disabled in cities, of which 87,000 were under the quota system. However, the implementation of the quota system in the past few years has not been fully satisfactory and data indicate that the number of persons employed under the quota system has been small. From 2003 to 2007, the number of disabled people that were newly employed under the quota system was 84,000, 88,000, 114,000, 99,000, and 115,000,

[5] *The Law on Protection of Persons with Disabilities*, Articles 31, 32.

[6] China Disabled Persons' Federation (CDPF): *Statistical Bulletin of Disabled Persons' Undertakings in China, 2013*. http://www.cdpf.org.cn/sjzx/tjgb/201403/t20140331_357749.shtml.

[7] *The Law on Protection of Persons with Disabilities*, Article 33.

[8] *The Employment Regulations for the Disabled (2007)*, Article 8.

[9] *The Employment Regulations for the Disabled (2007)*, Article 9.

respectively.[10] In reality, many enterprises did not reach the quota for hiring the disabled. Across the country, the number of people with disabilities who were employed in cities and towns reach 4.456 million in 2013; and the number for rural areas was 17.572 million, including 13.854 million in agriculture.[11] However, the employment rate for the disabled is not high. According to a statistics, in 2013, there were 37.3 % persons with disabilities who can take care of themselves in daily life in urban areas got employed and 47.3 % in rural areas.[12]

In recent years, the government has become more aware of its special responsibilities in combating disability discrimination and in promoting employment for the disabled. Great efforts have been made in this regard. In 2008, the central government issued the *Opinion on Promoting Undertakings for the Disabled*, which clearly instructed that the government agencies, public institutions and state-owned enterprises should take the lead in offering job opportunities for the disabled. In 2013, seven government agencies, including the Ministry of Human Resources and Social Security and China Disabled Persons' Federation, jointly issued another *Opinion on Promoting the Quota System for the Employment of the Disabled* (the "*Opinion*").

According to the *Opinion* in 2013, government agencies, public institutions, and state-owned enterprises must play an exemplary role in hiring and providing employment for the disabled. When recruiting for jobs that can be performed adequately by the disabled, preferential consideration should be accorded a candidate with a disability if s/he is otherwise on a par with one with no disability. Government at all levels must firmly safeguard the right of the disabled to apply for civil servant positions. Apart from very special posts, there should be no extra eligibility requirements for people with disabilities. The *Opinion* also pointed out that those employers that fail to fulfill the quota requirements must pay into *the Fund* strictly according to the regulation.

Second, subsidies, incentives, and penalties for employers should be strengthened. The *Opinion* laid out social security subsidies that will be given to qualified employers who provide employment for the disabled. More reward from *The Fund* can be offered to the employers that provide employment for the disabled according to or exceeding the quota.

The *Opinion* will promote employment for the disabled since it emphasizes the leading role of government agencies and state-owned enterprises, and enhanced incentives and penalties. But as the *Opinion* only provides guideline and is not a formal statute, and there is no strong mechanism for implementation. The effect of its implementation remains to be seen.

---

[10] China Disabled Persons' Federation (CDPF): *Situation of Disabled Persons' Undertakings in China, 2003–2007 – Employment and Social Security.* CDPF website: http://www.cdpf.org.cn/special/2008-5daihui/content/2008-11/07/content_30178596.htm.

[11] China Disabled Persons' Federation (CDPF): *Statistical Bulletin of Disabled Persons' Undertakings in China, 2013.*

[12] *The Monitoring Report of the Situations of the Disabled and their Well-off Process*, http://www.cdpf.org.cn/sjzx/jcbg/201408/t20140812_411000.shtml.

4.2.2 *Defects of the Quota System*

Using the quota system to promote the employment of the disabled is a social policy that has been adopted in many countries. However, it has both positive and negative effects. In China, where public awareness of equal opportunity in employment is relatively weak, the effect of the quota system is especially worrisome.

First, to a certain degree, the quota system sacrifices the employer's freedom of recruitment. Requiring all government agencies, public institutions, and enterprises to adopt the quota system regardless of their specific situations (including job availability and candidates' competency) imposes restrictions and burdens on them in regard to hiring. Also, uniform imposition of the quota requirement across different industries and sectors appears unfair. Moreover, the system is mandatory, and employers that fail to reach the quota requirement have to pay into the *Fund*, which will be a burden to some employers.

Second, the quota system itself does not ensure equal rights to employment for the disabled. Once the quota is reached, some employers may stop hiring qualified persons with disabilities, which might constitute discrimination against the disabled. Also since payment into the *Fund* is an alternative to hiring the disabled, some employers may opt for it and avoid the latter. This does not help foster respect for the disabled in the society as a whole or protect their rights to employment.

Third, the cost of enforcement of the quota system is relatively high since enforcement will be carried out by administrative agencies and the number of employers is huge. Ensuring fair allocation of limited job positions among the disabled is also difficult. How to collect contribution toward the *Fund*, and how to effectively use and manage the *Fund* are by no means easy issues. These have become urgent and important issues, since the *Fund* is growing rapidly.

Fourth, the quota system can hardly ensure that the disabled will enjoy equal treatment at work. Since the employer has to pay into the *Fund* if they do not hire any or enough disabled people, when they do hire disabled people, they may be doing so unwillingly. This may place the disabled they hire at a disadvantage due to a lack of trust and cooperation. Moreover, employers who hire the disabled only in order to avoid paying into the *Fund* may fail to provide good working condition or suitable positions, or to give equal treatment to the disabled, and may give them only low-status and low-paying jobs to do.

In short, the quota system could easily make the employer treat the duty of hiring the disabled as a mere obligation owed to the government. This is not conducive to fostering the culture of equal treatment for the disabled. And when the disabled are treated unfavorably, under the quota system, they often do not have access to remedies. Therefore, without the antidiscrimination law, it is difficult for the quota system itself to promote employment for and equal treatment of the persons with disabilities.

4.3 Relationship Between Anti-discrimination Law and the Quota System

In many countries, in addition to the quota system for the disabled, there is also anti-discrimination legislation. The relationship between the two is complex. Each has their strengths and weaknesses. Anti-discrimination legislation can claim some advantages over the quota system in the following respects:

First, anti-discrimination laws are conducive to protecting the equal right to employment of the disabled in that the law gives the disabled the right to sue when they are discriminated against, and the disabled can use the law for self-protection. This is in contrast to the quota system, under which employees or job seekers with disabilities usually have no recourse to adequate remedies if the employer does not fulfill their obligation. The implementation of the quota system mainly relies on the government agencies rather than the parties in any labor relationship.

Second, anti-discrimination laws are more flexible and strike the right balance between protecting the equal rights of the disabled to employment and protecting the employer's rights and autonomy in hiring. In anti-discrimination laws, only those disabled who are qualified for any particular job position are protected, and the employer does not have a duty to employ unqualified persons with disabilities. Also, the employer does not have a duty to meet the quota for disability hires, which helps to protect their interests. But the employer does have a duty to provide reasonable accommodation to facilitate the employment of the disabled, which reflects public policy and the employer's social responsibility to the disabled. In this way, anti-discrimination laws take both the interests of the employer and the disabled employee or job seeker into consideration.

Third, anti-discrimination laws are conducive to establishing a relationship of equality between the employer and the employee. Since no one is subject to a quota requirement, it makes it easier to establish trust, cooperation, and equality between the two.

Fourth, anti-discrimination laws are conducive to overcoming the defects of the quota system. Since there is no quota requirement, the employer can hire as many persons with disabilities and provide them with equal treatment as there are qualified candidates with disabilities instead of simply to meet an arbitrary quota.

Fifth, anti-discrimination laws have lower administrative enforcement cost than the quota system. The enforcement of anti-discrimination laws mainly relies on the victims of discrimination. However, the implementation of the quota system involves the daily monitoring, fee collection and management of administrative agencies. Therefore, the enforcement costs of anti-discrimination law are relatively lower.

Of course, the anti-discrimination system also has its disadvantages. Because anti-discrimination law in employment is not administratively coercive, their enforcement mainly relies on voluntary compliance by the employer and the victims' acts of self-defense through litigation. When the employer lacks the notion of employment equality, the employee lacks awareness of their rights and the availability of remedies, and the court lacks the adequate authority and ability to interpret the law and properly handle the cases, it would be difficult to effectuate the legislative intent of anti-discrimination law. The frequent occurrence of flexible and difficult concepts such as "disability", "qualified", "essential functions of the job", and "reasonable accommodation" in anti-discrimination law makes this even more so. Interpreting and enforcing these concepts requires high levels of competency of the court, which is a still a big challenge in China's court system today.

Considering the pressure of unemployment and the huge number of the disabled, and the lack of awareness of employment equality on the part of the society as a whole, it is necessary to continue the quota system. Since the quota system is mandatory and those that fail to comply must pay a penalty, it produces immediate effects in promoting employment for the disabled. But as mentioned above, it also has obvious defects: employers may either hire only as many people with disabilities as would meet the quota requirement or even opt to pay a penalty instead of hiring the disabled. Anti-discrimination law can correct these defect by requiring that as long as a person with a disability qualifies for a job, the employer must perform the duty of non-discrimination without reference to any quota requirement. While anti-discrimination law focus on an employer's recognition of and respect for the equal rights of the disabled, the quota system focuses on the employer's obligation to the government to hire the disabled. Combination of the two could enable the employer to fulfill the obligation imposed by the government of hiring the disabled while at the same time respecting disabled persons' equal right to employment. Given the current situation in China, the two approaches can go hand-in-hand to complement each other, i.e., the anti-discrimination mechanism can be an important instrument for implementing the quota system.

4.4 How to Improve the System of Anti-discrimination Against Disability in China

China's current legislation on anti-discrimination in employment are overly simplistic, contain no definitive criteria for deciding when discrimination has occurred, and few clear rules about the redress for discrimination. These laws provide inadequate protection for the disabled. Future legislation and case laws should make the following clear: what "disability" means, what criteria are applicable for determining whether a person with a disability is competent for a job, the employer's grounds for self-defense, whether the employer has a duty to accommodate the disabled employee and if so, the scope of that duty, what remedies should be available for the victims, who has the burden of proof, and which government agencies are in charge of combating disability discrimination, and so forth. Much can be learned from the *Americans with Disabilities Act* (ADA) in the U.S. Chinese legislators can try to introduce into the anti-discrimination laws such concepts as "disability", "qualified," "essential functions of the job," and "reasonable accommodation" can be introduced. In light of the experience of the US and other countries, an employer cannot refuse to hire a person with a "disability", as long as the person can perform "essential functions of the job," and the employer has a duty to make "reasonable accommodation" to enable the employed to perform "essential functions of the job."

The employer's duty to make "reasonable accommodation" is of special importance in anti-discrimination law. The Directive of the European Union also requires member states to legally prohibit discrimination against the disabled and employers to recognize their duty to make "reasonable accommodation."[13] "Reasonable accommodation" is a unique concept in disability discrimination law. This duty of the employer is crucial in ensuring equal treatment in employment for the disabled. British scholars have observed that the duty of reasonable accommodation is a core element in the latest measures adopted in many countries for eliminating disability discrimination and one that is based on the notion of human rights. This duty originated from the realization that only by providing reasonable accommodation for the disabled can they actually exercise their ability to work, and only then can the goal of equal treatment be achieved.[14] As for the burden of proof in this regard, it is the employee's duty to provide *prima facie* evidence of having requested reasonable accommodation and to establish the feasibility of requested accommodation; then the burden of proof falls on the employer to show that the duty of reasonable accommodation cannot be fulfilled.[15]

China has similar concept in the *Law on Protection of Persons with Disabilities*, which stipulates that "the employer of persons with disabilities should provide appropriate working conditions and labor protections and make adjustments in the workplace, working equipment, and living facilities according to the condition of the disabled employee and the requirements of the situation."[16] This provision is similar to the "reasonable accommodation" duty in the other countries, but it still has the following ambiguities and defects.

First, the subject of the provision is "the employer of a disabled employee," which seems to imply that this provision is only applicable to an employer that has already hired employees with disabilities. It is not clear whether the employer has a duty to make such accommodation for the disabled job seekers during recruitment process. Second, the provision stipulates that improvements should be made according to the actual requirements of the situation. It is not clear what constitutes "actual requirements" and no clear criteria are provided. Also, this provision only concerns the needs of the disabled employee, and does not take the ability of or costs to the

[13] Article 5, Council Directive 2000/78, Establishing a General Framework for Equal Treatment in Employment and Occupation.

[14] Catherine Barnard, *EC Employment Law*, Third Edition, Oxford University Press, 2006, p. 401.

[15] Mark A. Rothstein, Charles B. Craver, Elinor P. Schroeder, Elaine W. Shoben, *Employment Law*, Third Edition, West, 2005, p. 315.

[16] *The Law on Protection of the Disabled,* Article 38, Sec. 3.

employer into consideration. This may impose an unreasonable burden on the employer. Third, it is unclear if an employer's failure to perform their duty to "make adjustments" constitutes discrimination, or violation of the quota system, and if so, what the employer should be liable for. These questions have yet to be clearly answered. Chinese legislators can learn from the legislative experience and cases in European countries and the U.S. in their effort to formulate clear criteria for the duty of "reasonable accommodation" and the employer's legal liabilities in cases of failure to fulfill this duty.

Chapter 5
Wages, Work Hours and Holidays

5.1 Wage System in General

5.1.1 Definition of Wage

"Wage" means remuneration directly paid to the employee by the employer in the form of cash in accordance with relevant government regulations or the labor contract. "Wage" generally can encompass hourly wage, wage by piecework, bonuses, allowances, subsidies, overtime pay, and remuneration under special circumstances. Wage constitutes the majority of an employee's income. According to the regulations, the following employee income is not considered wage: (1) benefits paid to individual employees by the employer, such as bereavement benefits, hardship relief, and family planning subsidies; (2) supplies for labor protection, such as work uniforms, antidotes, and beverages; (3) other remunerations and earning not included in an employee's total income, such as legitimate award money associated with such honors as the Invention Award, the National Spark Award, the Natural Science Award, the Science and Technology Progress Award, the Sound Technical Improvements Proposal Award, and the China Skills Grand Award, as well as royalties for scripts, lecture fees, and translation fees.[1]

According to China's *Labor Law*, "wages should be paid to the employee monthly in the form of cash."[2] As the mode of employment becomes more diversified, the forms of wage payment have become more flexible. Some regulations permit the employer to pay remuneration in the form of hourly, daily, weekly or monthly wages. If wages are assignment-based, it should be paid to the employee immediately after the assignment is completed. But wages should be disbursed at least once every month.[3]

---

[1] Ministry of Labor, *Opinions on Issues Regarding Implementation of the Labor Law of the People's Republic of China,* Article 53.

[2] *Labor Law,* Article 50.

[3] *Regulations of Wage Payment in Beijing*, Article 9.

Z. Xie, *Labor Law in China*, Research Series on the Chinese Dream and China's Development Path, DOI 10.1007/978-3-662-46929-3_5

5.1.2 Principles of Remuneration and Determination of Wages

According to the *Labor Law*, the two basic principles for setting the wage are: (1) to each according to his contribution; and (2) equal pay for equal work.[4] Although these two principles are quite unambiguous conceptually, their implementation is rather difficult. The two principles usually apply when we are discussing a single employer. Since the job position and performance of individual employees varies widely, implementation of the two principles is not easy. In reality, there are few cases arguing the principle of "equal pay for equal work", and even fewer cases where the plaintiffs win the cases.[5] This goes to show how difficult it can be to implement this principle.

Also, according to the *Labor Law*, "the employer shall determine its wage distribution form and wage level according to law and to its own business operation and earning situation."[6] This indicates that the employer primarily set its wages without much government interference. Wage levels are primarily the result of negotiations between the employer and the employee and are an important factor in the competition of the labor market in which the government should avoid excessive interference. Except for the control on the salary of some high corporate executives in state-owned enterprises, the wages of employees in most enterprises are agreed to by the employees and the employers themselves.

In recent years, China has seen a rapid growth of workers' wages because of the significant demographic changes. The working-age population of people between 15 and 59 years old started to decline in 2011, which means changes in the labor supply and demand. As there has been labor shortage in some labor-intensive sectors, the average wages have increased sharply, whose growth rate was much higher than that of GDP. For example, in 2009–2012, the average yearly increase rate of the wages of migrant workers was 17.4 %, while the growth rate of GDP was 9.2 %.[7] The change of labor market provides a good opportunity for better working condition including the increase of wages.

5.1.3 Major Regulations on Wages

The following are the main restrictions on wages imposed by government regulations:

---

[4] *Labor Law*, Article 46.

[5] Feifei Ke, Yanlong Jiang, and Tiancheng Jiang, *Analysis on the Difficulty in the Cases concerning the Principle of "Equal Work, Equal Pay" Brought by the Dispatch Workers*, China Labor, 2011, No.12, p. 19.

[6] *Labor Law*, Article 47.

[7] Fang Cai, *The Dilemma of Wage Raise: To Interfere or to Correct the Market?* In Fang Cai (ed.): China Population and Labor Report, No. 14: From Demographic Dividend to Institutional Dividend, Social Sciences Academic Press, 2013, p. 82, 86.

First, wage under special circumstances. According to the law: "the employer should pay wages to the employee according to the law during legal holidays, wedding and bereavement leave, and legitimate social activities."[8] In addition, according to relevant government regulations maternity leave and family visit leave must be paid. How sick leave and leave for personal needs are handled is also an important part of the wage system. For instance, under the regulations of the Beijing municipality, during an employee's sick leave or non-work related injury, the employer should pay wages to the employee according to their labor contract or their collective contract. Wages during sick leave should not be lower than 80 % of the minimum wage of the municipality. The employer does not have to pay wages when the employee is taking leave for personal needs.[9] An employee is not providing labor service when sick, so theoretically the employer does not need to pay wages. But as a matter of social policy, the law requires that the employer pay partial wages. But for personal leave other than sickness, it is reasonable that the employer does not have to pay remuneration.

Second, overtime pay. The overtime pay standard in Chinese labor law is quite advantageous toward the employees. According to the *Labor Law,* the employer must pay the employee no less than 150 % of their regular wage for overtime work. When the employer requests the employee work overtime during the employee's day off, and the employee cannot make up for the loss, the employer must pay no less than 200 % of the regular wage. When the employee is requested to work during official holidays, the pay should be no less than 300 % of the regular wage.[10] The overtime pay standard in China is higher than in many countries where the overtime pay is normally 150 % of the regular wage. This is favorable toward the employees, but it also makes some employers unwilling to pay or fail to pay the required amount of overtime wages, which has caused many labor disputes related to overtime pay.

Third, the minimum wage system. An analysis of the minimum wage system is detailed below.

5.2 The Minimum Wage

To receive a fair wage is a basic right of the employee. The pros and cons of the minimum wage system have been subject to on-going debate. Even in Europe, some countries still do not have a minimum wage standard, and some countries only adopted the minimum wage system quite recently. For instance, in the U.K., there had been no general minimum wage system until the National Minimum Wage Act was implemented in 1998.

---

[8] *Labor Law,* Article 51.

[9] *Regulations of Wage Payment in Beijing*, Articles 21, 22.

[10] *Labor Law,* Article 44.

5.2.1 Theories and Debates on the Minimum Wage System

From an economic perspective, the invisible hand of the market would automatically adjust the wage. If no other factors are involved, the wage and the employer's demand for the employee are inversely correlated. The market will adjust to the demand for and the supply of labor to reach a balance. The wage at that point of equilibrium will be the equilibrium wage. Those economists who are against the minimum wage hold that: (1) with the increase in labor costs, the employer will hire fewer workers, and the minimum wage system will result in many people, especially the vulnerable, losing their jobs; (2) with wage increases, more and more people will want to enter the labor market, which will cause more unemployment; (3) the minimum wage will lead to low allocation efficiency. Those who would lose jobs because of the minimum wage requirement could not continue to work or could only work in occupations where the minimum wage requirement does not apply. Thus, these workers cannot "fully utilize their abilities," which is a loss to society as a whole.[11]

The main argument in favor of the minimum wage is the negative impact of cheap labor on productive efficiency. These economists believe that cheap labor will lead to low efficiency of organization and management, delay the replacement of outdated production equipment, and result in destructive price competition. The lack of minimum wage protections could result in the persistence of enterprises that are backward in technology and management. This will hinder more advanced enterprises from expanding their market share, thus decreasing the average level of productivity and impeding introduction of new technologies and new products. Furthermore, unfair income distribution caused by low wages will have a negative impact on consumer spending level and pattern. Therefore, from the perspective of social justice, equality, and civilized society, a minimum wage protection system is necessary. It will put pressure on employers to improve management, technology, and products, improve training and HR policies so as to unleash workers' potentials, and promote economic growth and employment opportunities.[12]

In general, whether to establish a minimum wage system depends on the structure and function of the labor market and the respective roles of the government and the market in the labor relationship. Moreover, the minimum wage system is closely linked to other systems such as the trade union and collective bargaining mechanism, and its relative strength. In countries where trade unions and collective bargaining mechanisms are strong, minimum wage systems will be less significant, because trade unions will help workers obtain reasonable wages.

---

[11] A.C.L. Davies: *Perspectives on Labor Law*, Cambridge University Press, 2004, pp. 138–139.

[12] See Huge Collins, K.D. Ewing and Aileen McColgan, *Labor Law: Text and Materials*, Hart Publishing, Oxford and Portland, Oregon, 2005, pp. 389–391.

5.2.2 *Main Points of the Minimum Wage System*

5.2.2.1 The Background of China's Minimum Wage System

The first Chinese law on labor, the *Labor Law,* was enacted in 1994. Within less than 10 years, in 2003, the *Minimum Wage Regulations* was adopted. Even though the history of Chinese labor law is relatively short, China's minimum wage system has been rigorously enforced. There are multiple reasons for this. First, in China's labor market, supply exceeded demand and wages were very low for quite a long time. In order to protect workers' basic rights, it was necessary to enforce a minimum wage. Second, as mentioned, China has a huge population of migrant workers from rural areas, which reached 26.894 million in 2013.[13] With low education levels and job skills, and great mobility, their rights and interests are vulnerable to violations. Enforcing a minimum wage would provide better protection for them. Third, collective bargaining mechanisms are not strong in China and it is difficult for workers to receive wage raises through collective bargaining. So, imposing a minimum wage system has a positive impact.

The minimum wage system appears to be a minor detail in labor law, yet it involves quite a few theoretical and practical issues, such as the minimum wage standard, eligible workers, definition and scope of wages, calculation methods, and enforcement and remedies. The *Minimum Wage Regulations* addressed these issues, as did the *Labor Law* and the *Labor Contract Law.*

5.2.2.2 Main Components of the Minimum Wage System

1. Scope. The minimum wage system is applicable to enterprises and individually-owned businesses, and the employees in these enterprises and businesses.[14]
2. The forms of minimum wage. Minimum wage standards include minimum monthly wages applicable to full-time employees, and minimum hourly wages applicable to part-time employees.[15]
3. Basis for determination and adjustment of minimum wages. When determining and adjusting the standard of a minimum monthly wage, factors to be considered in a particular locality should include: the minimum living cost for local workers and the number of family members that they support; urban and township consumer price index; the amount payment toward social insurance and housing provident fund; the average wage of local employees; and the local economic development and employment situation.[16]

---

[13] Ministry of Human Resources and Social Security, *Statistical Bulletin of the Development of Human Resources and Social Security Undertaking of 2013.*

[14] *The Minimum Wage Regulations,* Article 2.

[15] *The Minimum Wage Regulations,* Article 5.

[16] *The Minimum Wage Regulations,* Article 6.

4. The agencies that set the minimum wage standards and areas applicable. The minimum wage standards and adjustment proposals are drafted by labor administrative agencies at the provincial level. Draft proposals are shared with the equivalent-level trade union organization and enterprise association or entrepreneur's society, then submitted to the Human Resource and Social Security Ministry. The Ministry may propose revisions, and if there are no responses within 14 days after the local government submits the proposal, the proposal will be deemed accepted and effective. Different administrative areas at the provincial level can have different minimum wage standards. In addition, the minimum wage standards must be adjusted at least every two years.[17]
5. Scope of wages. When determining whether a worker's wage complies with the minimum wage standard, the following are not considered the components of a wage: overtime pay, midday shift and night shift pay, and allowances for working under extraordinary conditions, such as in extreme temperatures, in underground mine shafts, and under toxic and hazardous conditions. In addition, benefits provided to the employee in accordance with the law, regulation, and government provisions are not counted as wages.[18]
6. Implementation. The employer must make the minimum wage standards known to all its employees within 10 days of the standards being promulgated. In any case where current the wage paid by the employer is lower than the minimum wage, the labor administrative agency shall order the employer to make up all back pay owed to the worker in full. The administrative agency may also order the employer to pay compensation, which can be one to five times the wage owed to the employee.[19]

5.2.2.3 Implementation of the Minimum Wage System

In the past decades, for quite a long time, unskilled workers in labor-intensive enterprises received low wages. But the labor market has seen some changes, and minimum wage standards have increased remarkably in recent years. In 2012, 25 provincial-level local governments adjusted their minimum wage standards, with an average increase of 20.2 %. The highest monthly minimum wage was in Shenzhen, at 1,500 yuan, and the highest hourly minimum was in Beijing, at 14 yuan.[20] In 2013, 27 provincial level local governments raised the minimum wage standards, with an average increase of 17 %. In 2013, the highest monthly minimum wage in the country was 1,620 yuan in Shanghai, and the highest minimum hourly wage was

[17] *The Minimum Wage Regulations*, Article 7, 8, 10.

[18] *The Minimum Wage Regulations*, Article 12.

[19] *The Minimum Wage Regulations*, Article 11, 12.

[20] Ministry of Human Resources and Social Security, *Statistical Bulletin of the Development of Human Resources and Social Security Undertaking of 2012*.

15.2 yuan in Beijing and Xinjiang.[21] Such high increases were partly due to the government's efforts to strengthen labor protection. In addition, as mentioned above, structural changes in China's labor market in recent years have also played an important role. The Lewis turning point occurred in China in 2004, and starting, the labor force population within the age range of 15–59 began to see negative growth in 2011. This demographic change reflected the short supply of labor in general. It became increasingly difficult for enterprises to find workers, which drove the minimum wage up sharply.[22] Labor-intensive types of enterprises had an especially hard time recruiting workers, and their wages went up faster. For example, in 2011, the average annual wage of workers employed by private enterprises in cities and towns was 24,556 yuan, showing an 18.3 % increase over 2010.[23] In 2012, the average annual wage of these workers was 28,752 yuan, a 17.1 % increase over 2011.[24] In 2013, the average annual wage of these workers was 32,706 yuan, a 13.8 % increase over 2012.[25] An increase of the average wage naturally led to an increase in the minimum wage.

5.2.3 Problems in and Improvements Needed for China's Minimum Wage System

Compared to the minimum wage systems in some other countries and regions, the system in China has a number of defects that should be corrected. They are as follows.

First, which government department is charged with setting the minimum wage should be more clearly defined, and their methodology should improve. The determination of the minimum wage should be based on comprehensive consideration of various factors, and the weighing of all pros and cons, and only a body or organization with the appropriate expertise and relevant authority can assume this serious responsibility. According to the *Minimum Wage Regulations,* the provincial level labor department drafts the minimum wage standards proposal in consultation with the provincial trade union and enterprise organizations. It is then submitted to the provincial government for approval. Thus, the final decision-making power for the

[21] Ministry of Human Resources and Social Security, *Statistical Bulletin of the Development of Human Resources and Social Security Undertaking of 2013.*

[22] Fang Cai, *The Dilemma of Wage Raise: To Interfere or to Correct the Market?* In Fang Cai (ed.), China Population and Labor Issues Report, No. 14: From Demographic Dividend to Institutional Dividend, Social Sciences Academic Press, 2013, p. 82.

[23] Ministry of Human Resources and Social Security, *Statistical Bulletin of the Development of Human Resources and Social Security Undertaking f of 2011.*

[24] Ministry of Human Resources and Social Security, *Statistical Bulletin of the Development of Human Resources and Social Security Undertaking of 2012.*

[25] Ministry of Human Resources and Social Security, *Statistical Bulletin of the Development of Human Resources and Social Security Undertaking of 2013.*

minimum wage lies with the provincial government. An important issue then is how to settle the matter when the labor department and the trade union or enterprise organization have different opinions.

In some countries, a relatively independent entity is established to be responsible for consultations and recommendations for the minimum wage. For instance, in the U.K., according to the 1998 Act, the Secretary of State promulgates the minimum wage standards in the form of regulations. And the government set up a Low Pay Commission responsible for consultations and recommendations concerning the minimum wage standards.[26] This Commission is a non-departmental public body. The U.K.'s approach is worth considering. In China, local legislatures, i.e., the local People's Congresses, can play an important role when there are major disagreements among the provincial labor department, trade union, and enterprise organization.

Second, a uniform national minimum wage standard does not yet exist.

In China, the decision-making power to set the minimum wage rests with the provincial governments (and some cities have the authority to implement their own standard). In order to promote the universal adoption of the minimum wage, it is necessary to set a national minimum wage standard, while at the same time allowing provincial governments to set their own minimum wage standards as long as they are no lower than the national standard. Even in a country as big as the United States, there is a uniform national minimum wage standard.[27] In China, a uniform n standard seems necessary.

Third, the current minimum wage standard is too low.

In developed countries the minimum wage is usually 40–60 % of the average wage, whereas the minimum wage in China is far below this. Taking Beijing as an example, in 2012, the average annual wage of workers in the city was 62,677 yuan, and average monthly wage was 5,223 yuan.[28] But in the same year, the minimum monthly wage in Beijing was 1,260 yuan,[29] which is only 24.1 % of the average wage, which is very low. The minimum wage standard being too low is also an important factor contributing to the large wage gap and disparity between different groups.

Four, the criteria for determining whether the minimum wage requirement has been complied with are not clear.

1. Although the minimum wage system in China includes a minimum monthly wage and minimum hourly wage, it does not have the pay reference period that is common in some other countries. The function of a pay reference period is to ensure that the worker's wage is not lower than the minimum wage in every pay

---

[26] Http://www.lowpay.gov.uk/. The Low Pay Commission (LPC) was established as a result of the *National Minimum Wage Act 1998* to advise the Government about the National Minimum Wage.

[27] *Fair Labor Standards Act*, Sec. 6.

[28] Source: Beijing City Statistics Information website: http://www.bjstats.gov.cn/tjzn/mcjs/201306/t20130608_250284.htm.

[29] Source: Beijing City Human Resources and Social Security Bureau website, *Relevant Standards of Social Security in Beijing of the Past Years,* http://www.bjstats.gov.cn/tjzn/mcjs/201306/t20130608_250284.htm.

reference period. Employers are not allowed to use the average wage of a longer period beyond the pay reference period as the criterion for determining whether the minimum wage standard has been honored. This pay reference period is especially important for the protection of workers whose income is unstable and based on a piece-work wage. Since most employers in China pay wages on a monthly basis, the pay reference period in China should be one month.

2. Both the minimum monthly wage and minimum hourly wage should be applicable to full-time employees. According to the *Minimum Wage Regulations,* the monthly minimum wage standard is applicable to full-time employees and the minimum hourly wage standard to other employees. In some countries, the minimum wage standard is usually the minimum hourly wage regardless of the employee's work status. This is because the work hours of full-time workers vary widely and a monthly minimum wage does not reflect the difference among workers in terms of the number of days and/or hours they work. For instance, both the US and the U.K. use the minimum hourly wage standard. Therefore, in China, both the minimum monthly wage and minimum hourly wage should be applicable to full-time employees.
3. The *Minimum Wage Regulations* does not give a clear definition of the types of income that should not be counted in minimum wage calculations. Article 12 of the *Regulations* only excluded certain income, such as overtime pay, allowances for special work conditions, and benefits provided by the government in compliance with laws and regulations. It is not clear whether some other forms of remuneration should be included in the minimum wage calculation, such as room and board, payment in kind, and vouchers provided by the employer. It is especially important to make sure that the employer is not avoiding the duty of paying the minimum wage when room and board is provided. Hence, the criteria for deciding whether the minimum wage requirement has been complied with should be improved in China.

Fifth, the administrative enforcement measures and mechanisms for making the minimum wages public should be improved.

Article 11 of China's *Minimum Wage Regulations* stipulates that the employer should make these facts known to all employees within 10 days of the promulgation of the minimum wage standard. This provision does not make it clear when and how many times the notice should be made, so it does not guarantee that all employees are aware of the minimum wage standard. The law should require the employer to make the minimum wage standard known to the workers when the labor contract is signed. This will ensure that the worker receives the information.

As for the enforcement measures of administrative agencies, Article 13 of the *Minimum Wage Regulations* stipulates that, in cases that the employer does not comply with the minimum wage, the labor administrative agency shall order the employer to pay back wages owed to the worker within a certain period of time. The administrative agency may also order the employer to pay a compensation that is one to five times the wages owed to the employee. Since not paying the minimum wage is a serious violation of the law, apart from ordering the violator to make up the shortfall, the administrative agency should also be given the power to levy a penalty on the employer. However, the provision that the administrative agency "may also order the employer to pay compensation amounting to one to five times the wages owed to the employee" seems to give the administrative agency overly broad discretion.

Sixth, an employer's liability for violating the minimum wage requirement is unclear. In Chinese law, the provisions pertaining to the employer's liabilities for violating the minimum wage system are scattered and inconsistent.

Article 14 of the *Minimum Wage Regulations* stipulates that disputes over the minimum wage between the employee and the employer should be treated according to labor disputes resolution provisions. According to Article 2 of the *Labor Dispute Mediation and Arbitration Law*, "labor remuneration" disputes include disputes about the minimum wage. Therefore, when the employee's remuneration is lower than the minimum wage standard, the worker can bring the case up for arbitration or sue in court. According to Article 85 of the *Labor Contract Law,* the labor administrative agency shall order the employer to make up the shortfall when the wage paid is lower than the local minimum wage. If back pay is not disbursed within the period ordered, the employer shall pay an additional 50–100 % of the makeup payment. But this provision only states the employer's liabilities for a violation from the point view of administrative enforcement, it does not indicate the compensation amount that the employee could ask for in arbitration or a lawsuit when their right to the minimum wage has been violated. In practice, the arbitration agency and the court usually do not support employee claims made according to Article 85 of the *Labor Contract Law*. In 2010, the Judicial Interpretation of the Supreme People's Court instructed the courts take the case when an employee press charge against an employer under Article 85 of the *Labor Contract Law*.[30] But the Supreme Court's instruction only required the courts to take those cases and did not state whether the courts should support the employee's claim.

In theory, failing to pay the minimum wage is a serious violation of the law. When it happens, no matter if an administrative agency is involved, the employer should not only pay back the shortfall but also pay additional compensation, and the compensation amount could be fixed in reference to Article 85 of the *Labor Contract Law*. This should be supported by the arbitration organs and courts.

5.3 Work Hours

5.3.1 Standard Work Hours

Regulation on work hours is an important part of labor law to protect the workers' health and rights. According to the *Labor Law*, The State shall practice a work hours system wherein employees shall work for no more than eight hours a day and

[30] *Interpretation of Applicable Laws in Adjudicating Labor Dispute Cases* by the Supreme People's Court (III), 2010, Article 3.

no more than 44 hours a week on average.[31] In 1995, the State Council revised a regulation and stipulated that employees shall work for no more than eight hours a day and no more than 40 hours a week.[32] This indicates that the rule of work hours in China is quite similar to those in many other countries.

5.3.2 Restrictions on Overtime

In addition to the rules governing work hours, the legislation in China also include strict rules on overtime hours and overtime wages. According to *Labor Law*, the employer may extend workers' work hours as necessitated by its production or business operation after consulting with the trade union and the employees, but the extension shall generally not exceed one hour each day; if such extension is needed for special reasons, under the condition that the health of employees is not under threat, the overtime shall not exceed three hours per day. However, the total overtime in a month shall not exceed 36 hours. However, under some exceptional and emergency situations, these limits may be allowably breached.[33] Generally speaking, Chinese law not only has strict provisions on the number of overtime hours, but it also requires the employer to follow certain procedures in such matters. Specifically, they must consult with the trade union and the concerned employee regarding overtime requests. Some scholars have argued that the restrictions are overly stringent and should be relaxed.[34] Moreover, as mentioned above, the Chinese law requires higher remuneration rates for overtime, which makes implementation difficult.

5.3.3 Special Work Hours Systems

Besides the standard work hours, to meet the needs of special enterprises and special positions, the law also provides for special work hours systems. If an enterprise cannot fulfill the standard work hours rules mentioned above, it can also adopt other work hours and rest and leave rules upon special an approval granted by the labor administrative agency.[35] According to the Regulation issued by the Ministry of Labor, an enterprise may, due to the need of operation, adopt the system of "flexible work hours" or the "aggregation system of work hours." upon the approval by the

[31] Article 36 of *Labor Law*, 1994.

[32] Article 3 of the *Regulations on Work Hours of the Employee*, 1995.

[33] Article 41, 42 of *Labor Law*.

[34] Wenzhen Wang, Kun Huang, *The Tasks and Countermeasures in the Labor Standards Legislation*, China Labor, 2012, No.5, p. 11.

[35] Article 39 of *Labor Law* of 1994.

administrative labor agency.[36] Under the Regulation, an enterprise can adopt the system of flexible work hours for the employee, such as corporate executives, auxiliary staff, sales personnel, staff on duty, and other employees for whom following standard work hours is difficult. The system of flexible work hours actually exempts an enterprise from having to comply with the standard work hour rules and the restrictions – in regard to both the number of hours and pay -in relation to overtime. As this system imposes no limit on the employees work hours, it only applies to specific posts and the employer has to obtain the approval of the local labor agency. And although no limits on work hours shall apply once this system has been adopted, the employer must still make sure that the employee's rights to health and rest are honored. Normally, if the employer adopts this special work hours, the employer will include this rule in the labor contracts. As the *Labor Law* has strict provisions on overtime, some argue the system of flexible work hours should apply to more employees and more posts; for example, this system should be applicable to those employees whose wages are more than three times the local average wages.[37]

Yet another work hour system is "aggregation system of work hours". Under this system, the number of hours worked is calculated by aggregating over a pre-determined period of time – it may be a week, a month, a quarter or a year – provided it is more or less consistent with the 8-hours-per-day and 40-hours-per-week standards. Otherwise, the employer has to pay for overtime. Under the regulation, the employer can apply for the system for the following types of employees: (a) those working in such industries as transportation, railways, telecommunications, shipping, aviation, fishery and others who need to work continuously for long periods of time due to the special nature of their work;(b) some of those working in geology and resource exploration, construction, salt and sugar production, tourism and other industries that are subject to seasonal variations and constrained by natural conditions; (c) other workers for whom such special work hours system is suitable.[38] The main characteristic of this system is that it enables workers to work and rest for extended periods of time due to the special requirement of the job.

With the rise of the service industry and greater flexibility in the modes of employment, more and more employers have asked to adopt the special work hour systems. For example, in Shanghai City, in 2007, only 7,089 employers adopted the systems for their employees; however, in 2008, the number grew to 11,949, an increase of 68 %.[39] Currently, there are still some defects in the rules that make up the special work hours system. First, as the national uniform rules on special work hours are couched in general terms, their implementation by local governments can

---

[36] Article 3 of the Measure concerning the approval on the system of flexible work hours and the aggregation system of work hours, No. 503, Issued by the Ministry of Labor, 1994.

[37] Wenzhen Wang, Kun Huang, *The Task and Countermeasures in the Labor Standards Legislation*, China Labor, 2012, No.5, p. 11.

[38] Article 5 of the Measure concerning the approval on the system of flexible work hours and the aggregation system of work hours, No. 503, Issued by the Ministry of Labor, 1994.

[39] Xinmin Zhang, *Suggestions for Improving the Special Work Hours system in China*, China Labor, 2012, No. 9, p. 6.

differ from place to place. Second, current rules on special work hours are too simplistic. There are no clear definitions on the system of "flexible work hours" and "aggregation system of work hours" or the posts or employees for which the two systems can be used. For example, although the Regulation stipulates that the system of "flexible work hours" can be used for corporate executives and auxiliary staff, but who counts as a "corporate executive" or a member of "auxiliary staff" remains unclear. Thirdly, there are no specific upper limits on work hours in certain period of time under the system of special work hours, which will be disadvantageous to the health and the right to rest of the employee. Fourthly, there are no detailed rules on the procedure for how the labor agencies reviews applications and grant approval for the two systems and how labor agencies should perform their supervisory duties. Therefore, the labor agencies sometimes approve the application submitted by the employers arbitrarily.[40]

5.4 Holidays

According to the *Labor Law*, the employer shall guarantee that their employees have at least one day off each week.[41] But the *Labor Law* remains silent the amount of break from work an employee is entitled to in each work day and the amount of break between two working days. Regarding public holidays, the *Labor Law* requires that the employer shall allow their employees to take days off on the following public holidays: New Year's day; Spring Festival; International Labor Day; National Day; and other holidays specified by the laws and regulations. The revised *Regulations on the Leave for the National Holidays and Memorial days* introduced in 2013 include the newest provisions regarding national holidays. According to this Regulations, national holidays for all citizens include New Year's Day, Spring Festival, Tomb Sweeping Day, Labor Day, Dragon Boat Festival, the Mid-Autumn Festival and National Day, amount to a total of 11 days.[42] Adjustments to the line-up of the public holiday were intended to honor China's traditional festivals. In addition, if the employer requires an employee to work during the public holidays, they have to pay three times the normal wage.

As for the annual vacation, the *Regulations on the Annual Paid Vacation for Workers* has detailed rules. According to this Regulations, workers who have worked continuously for more than one year are entitled to paid annual vacation. The employer should ensure that during their paid annual vacation their employees receive the same pay as they normally would, i.e., without any reduction.[43] As for the length of the annual vacation, it depends on the total number of years an

[40] Xinmin Zhang, *Suggestions for Improving the Special Work Hours System in China*, China Labor, 2012, No. 9, pp. 7–8.

[41] Article 38 of *Labor Law*.

[42] Article 2 of the *Regulations on the Leave for the National Holidays and Memorial Days* in 2013.

[43] Article 2 of the Regulations on the Annual Paid Vacation for Workers, 2007.

employee has worked since finishing school: 5 days for the employee who have worked for up to 10 years; 10 days for those who have worked for 10–20 years; 15 days for those who have worked for more than 20 years.[44] Compared with other countries, the paid vacation is too short. For example, in Germany, the law calls for an annual vacation of 24 business days, but in reality, in most sectors, the collective agreements will often grant annual vacation of 30 working days.[45] Another issue is whether the rule that the number of days an employee is entitled to for their annual vacation depends on how long they have been in the workforce constitutes age discrimination. Moreover, according to the Regulations, the employer should consider the wishes of the employee and make overall arrangements for the employees' vacation leaves based on the specific situation of production and work.[46] However, it still remains unclear how disagreements between the employer and the employee over the arrangement of the latter's annual vacation should be handled.

[44] Article 3 of the Regulations on the Annual Paid Vacation for Workers, 2007.

[45] Manfred Weiss and Marlene Schmidt, Labor Law and Industrial Relations in Germany, Kluwer Law International, 2008, p. 103.

[46] Article 5 of the Regulations on the Annual Paid Vacation for Workers, 2007.

Chapter 6
Regulation on Labor Dispatch

6.1 Labor Dispatch Legislation and Its Implementation

Labor dispatch has increased rapidly in China since the reform and opening-up policy was adopted. The main reason is that, for a long time, before the adoption of *Labor Contract Law* of 2007, no laws or regulations existed to govern this practice and many enterprises used dispatch workers to avoid employer's liabilities. In 2006, the All-China Federation of Trade Unions (ACFTU) estimated that there were approximately 25 million dispatched workers at that time.[1] Increase reliance on dispatched workers has created some problems: labor dispatch agencies arbitrarily withhold or deduct the wages of dispatch workers; many dispatched workers are paid less than others who do comparable work; many of them do not enjoy regular wage raises or promotions available to regular workers; many employers use more dispatched workers than justified to cut labor cost; and liability issues related to work-related injuries remain unclear.[2]

The *Labor Contract Law* of 2007 is the first piece of national legislation on labor dispatching. It included the following main provisions: the basic requirements for setting up a dispatch agency,[3] the contents of the contract both between the labor dispatch agency and the dispatched worker, and between the dispatch agency and the host company that uses the dispatched workers, dispatch agencies must sign fixed-term contracts valid for a minimum of two years with dispatched worker,[4] dispatch agencies must inform the dispatched worker of the content of the agreement they sign with the host company[5]; and contractual duties the dispatch agency and

[1] The All-China Federation of Trade Unions (ACFTU) Survey Group: *The Survey of China's Current Labor Dispatch Situation,* China Labor, 2012, No. 5, p. 23.

[2] Chunying Xin (ed.), *Interpretation of the Labor Contract Law of the People's Republic of China,* Law Press, 2007, pp. 211–212.

[3] *Labor Contract Law,* Article 57.

[4] *Labor Contract Law,* Article 58, 59.

[5] *Labor Contract Law,* Article 60.

Z. Xie, *Labor Law in China*, Research Series on the Chinese Dream and China's Development Path, DOI 10.1007/978-3-662-46929-3_6

the host company have toward each other.[6] According to this law, labor dispatch agencies have the legal status of "employers", and thus have the same duties toward the dispatched worker as would any regular employer. This law also clarifies the duties of the host company as follows: (1) providing proper work conditions and labor protection according to national labor standards; (2) informing the dispatched worker of their job duties and pay rate; (3) providing overtime pay, performance-based bonuses, and other fringe benefits related to the job; (4) providing essential on-the-job training for the dispatched workers according to the needs of the position; (5) giving regular raises to those dispatched worker who have worked continuously for the host employer.[7] The *Labor Contract Law* of 2007 also delineated the scope of the types of work eligible for labor dispatching, i.e., "in general, only temporary, supplementary, or substitute positions are eligible for the use of dispatched workers."[8] But this provision was meant as a guideline rather than binding.

Although the *Labor Contract Law* made provisions for labor dispatching, the current situation indicates that legislators' original intent of restricting and regulating the practice of labor dispatching has not been realized, even while the number of dispatched workers continues to rise sharply. According to ACFTU estimates, in 2011, the number of dispatched workers working in enterprises was about 37 million, accounting for 13.1 % of all employees working in enterprises in China. Other statistics show that the percentage was even higher in some localities.[9] As for the nature of the enterprises, state-owned enterprises are most dependent on dispatched workers, in which they account for 16.2 % of the total workforce; enterprises with foreign investment come in second, in which dispatched workers account for 14.0 % of their total workforce.[10]

Extensive use of dispatched workers has created many serious problems: (1) there are too many dispatch agencies and operational irregularities are widespread; (2) many employers use a large number of dispatched workers for extended periods of time, and some rely on it as their primary form of recruitment; (3) there is still no effective protection of the legitimate rights and interests of dispatched workers. Rights infringements are especially prominent in relation to the wage issue, where they are often paid less than their regular worker counterparts. Routinely denied the right to participate in enterprise management and to join trade unions, many dispatched workers lack a sense of belonging. The abusive use of dispatched workers has not only harmed the legitimate rights and interests of the workers themselves, but also negatively affected the regular recruitment practices of the labor contract

[6] *Labor Contract Law*, Article 58.

[7] *Labor Contract Law*, Article 62.

[8] *Labor Contract Law*, Article 66.

[9] The All-China Federation of Trade Unions (ACFTU) Survey Group: *The Survey of China's Current Labor Dispatch Situation*, China Labor, 2012, No. 5, p. 23.

[10] The All-China Federation of Trade Unions (ACFTU) Survey Group: *The Survey of China's Current Labor Dispatch Situation*, China Labor, 2012, No. 5, p. 23.

system.[11] The number of labor disputes related to labor dispatching has been on the rise in recent years. In other words, labor dispatching has not experienced orderly development in accordance with the expected objectives of the *Labor Contract Law*.

6.2 Main Reasons for Excessive Reliance on Labor Dispatch

Despite the *Labor Contract Law* having devoted a special section to the regulation of labor dispatching, the practice has become more widespread and the number of dispatched workers has continued to grow. Existing problems are worsening, at times threatening to render the law practically ineffectual. The overuse of labor dispatching could be due to the following factors.

6.2.1 Benefits of Labor dispatching

Its hidden economic benefits have driven the emergence and development of labor dispatching. This mode of employment satisfies the workers' need for flexible hours and reduces the cost and risks for the host company. And it can help improve division of labor and specialization in the labor market. For some specialized jobs such as security guards and construction workers, labor dispatch agencies can do what would be difficult or impossible for the host company that uses the dispatched workers to do, especially in relation to recruitment, screening, training, and HR management. Specialized services provided by labor dispatch agencies could reduce operations costs for the host company and improve efficiency of HR management and the level of specialization, which can enhance worker rights protection.[12]

In reality, some companies are using dispatched workers not to cut labor costs but to reduce the burden of HR management and to reduce employment risks. According to one survey, a considerable proportion of companies do not in fact think the use of dispatched workers necessarily lowers labor costs, because in addition to wages and insurances, fees must be paid to labor dispatch agencies.[13] Thus, labor dispatching is playing a positive role in enhancing employment and controlling risks for the employer. Because of these advantages of labor dispatching, companies have an incentive to use dispatched workers.

---

[11] National People's Congress (NPC) Law Committee, *Explanation of the Revision of the Labor Contract Law of the People's Republic of China (Draft)*, NPC website: http://www.npc.gov.cn/npc/xinwen/lfgz/flca/2012-07/06/content_1729107.htm.

[12] Zengyi Xie, *Labor Dispatch Laws and Regulations of the United States and Ideas for China's Labor Dispatch Legislation*, Comparative Law Study, 2007, No. 6, p. 104.

[13] Jinfeng Shi, *Study of Labor Dispatch Situation and Countermeasures*, People's Justice, 2009, No. 19, p. 17.

6.2.2 Insufficient Legal Regulation

Although the 2007 *Labor Contract Law* made provisions for labor dispatching, and demonstrated a legislative intent to restrict and regulate this practice, in reality, over a long period of time, non-regular forms of employment such as labor dispatching have been used by the government as an important means for promoting employment. No strict legal restrictions were imposed on labor dispatching in practice. Research has identified seven key elements of legal regulation of labor dispatching. They are: the scope of labor dispatch contract; the number of times that a labor dispatch contract can be renewed, and the total allowable duration of job positions using dispatched worker; terms of status change from dispatched worker to regular employee and non-fixed-term contract; the forms, registration and reportage requirements in relation to labor dispatching; and pay parity and work condition equality between dispatched workers and other workers. The research compared China's laws to relevant legislation in over forty countries and regions and came to the conclusion that the level of legal regulation of labor dispatching in China was relatively low by international standards.[14] I concur with the conclusion. Actually, restrictions on labor dispatching in the *Labor Contract Law* were too lax. The 2007 *Labor Contract Law* is significantly inadequate in relation to such important issues as the scope of eligibility for labor dispatching, renewal limits or the total duration of positions occupied by dispatched workers, mechanism for status change for dispatched worker into regular employee, regulations on labor dispatch agencies, enforcement mechanism for "equal pay for equal work" and monitoring mechanism.

6.2.3 Effect of the Labor Contract Law

The enactment of the 2007 *Labor Contract Law* enhanced labor protection standards in China. In particular, strict conditions for terminating a labor contract, and the requirement of non-fixed-term contracts prompted some enterprises to use dispatched workers to avoid relevant regulations regarding the labor contract. For example, according to one survey, when employers asked for their reasons for choosing to use dispatched workers, 29 % of the surveyed enterprises answered "to cut labor cost," and 21 % answered "to reduce risks of the *Labor Contract Law* compliance."[15] This indicates that the *Labor Contract Law* has a noticeable impact on corporation decision about the use of dispatched workers. Some employers are using it to cut labor costs and also to optimize management and to control the potential risks involved in recruitment and termination.

[14]Yefang Qian, *An International Comparison of Degree of Regulations on Labor Dispatch and Suggestions for China's Legislation*, Rule of Law Studies, 2012, No.5, p. 77.

[15]Ying Jiang, Xin Yang, *On Rights Protection of the Workers in Labor Dispatch – Based on Evidence Analysis of Labor Contract Law Questionnaires*, Academic Journal of National School of Administration, 2011, No.2, p. 54.

6.2.4 The Limit and Effect of Employment Modality

One striking phenomenon is that state-owned enterprises tend to be more reliant on dispatched workers compared with other kinds of employers. There are two reasons for this. First, the labor management system of state-owned enterprises has features that make the use of dispatched workers particular attractive to them. For instance, because they are subject to regulations about total payroll expenditure and allowable total number of employees, they are barred from expanding the size of their staff. Not only does the use of dispatched labor allow SOEs to circumvent both restrictions, just as importantly, the expenses associated with such practice can be written off as the cost of the enterprise to reduce taxes and other expenses related to employees.

Second, an inherent "duality" in employment structure continues to exist in traditional SOEs, where there is the distinction between formal and informal employees. There is a cap on the number of formal employees, who enjoy almost lifetime tenure with little job mobility. When more workers are needed, the enterprise will use dispatched workers to fill low-end support jobs. Formal employees enjoy higher wages and better benefits, whereas the large number of dispatched workers can only command market price wages. This leads to pay disparity between the two groups.

6.2.5 The Effect of the Urban–Rural Dual System

A survey by the ACFTU indicates that migrant workers from rural areas, and workers without local household registration accounted for 52.6 % of dispatched workers.[16] This indicates that the bulk of dispatched labor is made up of migrant workers, who are at a disadvantage due to their household registration status, education attainment levels, resource handicap and poor access to labor protection. For example, one survey shows that in 2010, the portion of migrant workers who had signed a labor contract with their employer was 38.88 percentage points lower than that for workers with local household registration.[17] In regard to the duration of the contract, one survey from 2009 to 2010 indicated that the portion of migrant workers who had signed fixed-term were 21.88 percentage points higher than that for urban workers, while the percentage of local urban workers who had signed non-fixed-term labor contracts were 24.65 percentage points higher than that for migrant workers.[18] This indicates that job stability is much higher for local urban workers than for

[16]The All-China Federation of Trade Unions (ACFTU) Survey Group: *The Survey of China's Current Labor Dispatch Situation,* China Labor, 2012, No. 5, p. 24.

[17]Meiyan Wang, *Implementation of Labor Contract Law: Problems and Countermeasure Suggestions,* Academic Journal of Guizhou College of Finance and Economics, 2013, No.1, p. 27.

[18]Meiyan Wang, *Implementation of Labor Contract Law: Problems and Countermeasure Suggestions,* Academic Journal of Guizhou College of Finance and Economics, 2013, No.1. pp. 27–28.

migrant workers. As many dispatch workers are migrant workers from rural areas and the imbalance of labor protection between urban and rural workers cannot be eliminated within a short period of time, neither will the achievement of the orderly development of labor dispatching and the full protection of dispatch workers.

6.3 The Problem of Unequal Pay for Equal Work

"Unequal pay for equal work" is generally regarded as the biggest problem in labor dispatching. "Currently the one right of dispatched workers that is most often infringed upon is that to equal pay for equal work."[19] Therefore, how to realize "equal pay for equal work" between dispatched workers and regular employees is a difficult and serious issue.

Although "equal pay for equal work" is a sound principle of justice that is universally accepted, compliance faces many challenges. As has been pointed out, "the principle of equal pay for equal work is compelling because of the fundamental legitimacy of the concept. Yet its full realization places high demands on the society in terms of both social conditions and institutional culture. In a non-ideal social environment, its inspirational value far exceeds its normative significance."[20] According to the *Explanation of Some Articles of the Labor Law* issued by the Ministry of Labor in 1994, "equal pay for equal work" requires the employer to pay all employees who do the same kind work, in the same amount and with the same result at the same rate.[21] Thus "equal pay for equal work" involves three requirements: first, the job positions and tasks must be the same; second, the amount of work must be the same; third, the result of the work must be the same. Somebody's job position and tasks are easy to determine, but the amount of work they do and the result of the work they do are harder to measure. Therefore, it is very difficult to determine precisely whether different employees are doing the "same type of work," "the same amount of work," and have achieved the "same work result." Therefore, it is very difficult to comply fully with the principle of "equal pay for equal work".

Internationally, the principle of equal pay for equal work first appeared in the *Equal Remuneration Convention of 1951*, which stated that "the term *equal remuneration for men and women workers for work of equal value* refers to rates of remuneration established without discrimination based on sex." This shows that equal pay for equal work originally mainly referred to equal remuneration between men and women. This was also true of legislation in some countries. For instance,

[19]Yongqian Tu, *Causes of Labor Dispatch Abuse and Legal Restrictions*, Forum of Political Science and Law, 2013, No.1, p. 179.

[20]Yanjun Feng, *Doubts and Reflections on the Principle of Equal Pay for Equal Work*, Studies of Law and Commerce, 2011, No. 2, p. 61.

[21]Ministry of Labor, *Explanations of Some Provisions of the Labor Law*, 1994, Article 46.

Britain adopted the *Equal Pay Act 1970*, which required that men and women workers of the "same employment" get "equal treatment."[22]

Some countries later applied the principle of equal pay for equal work between men and women to the framework of antidiscrimination legislation and its enforcement, which is conducive to the implementation of that principle. As time goes by, the issue of equal treatment of dispatched workers began to draw the attention of some legislators. In 2008, the European Union issued Council Directive No. 2008/104 on *Temporary Agency Work*. According to the document, equal treatment does not only apply to remuneration but also to work hours, overtime, breaks, holiday and vacation leaves, night shifts, and other employment terms and conditions.[23] This type of legislation and its implementation will help ensure realization of equal treatment for dispatched workers.

Compared to some countries, China still has a long way to go in non-discrimination legislation and practice. As mentioned above, relevant Chinese laws lack detailed provisions defining employment discrimination, the burden of proof, and available remedies for discrimination victims. Especially difficult is the absence of effective administrative agencies to enforce the regulations.[24] In reality, it is very difficult to implement employment non-discrimination law.[25] The goal of "equal pay for equal work" can hardly be realized under the current situation, where non-discrimination legislation and practice are both weak. In court cases, very few workers have won under the claim of "equal pay for equal work."[26] The full realization of this principle will take a long time.

6.4 The Revision of the Labor Contract Law in 2012

To address the problems in labor dispatching, the Chinese *Labor Contract Law* was revised in 2012, and some reform measures were introduced. Some of the most important ones are as follows:

First, the revision raised the bar for setting up a labor dispatch agency by increasing the amount of capital required for registration. Also, the requirement for an administrative license is imposed on those who wish to set up labor dispatch agencies. Only after the labor administrative agency issues the license, can a labor dispatch agency be legally registered.[27] In the past, the law only required labor dispatch

[22] *Equal Pay Act 1970,* Sec. 1.

[23] *Council Directive No. 2008/104 on Temporary Agency Work,* Articles 1, 3, 5.

[24] Timothy Webster, *Ambivalence and Activism: Employment Discrimination in China*, Vanderbilt Journal of Transnational Law, May, 2011, p. 705.

[25] Jiefeng Lu, *Employment Discrimination in China: the Current Situation and Principle Challenges*, Hamline Law Review, Winter, 2009, p. 189.

[26] Feifei Ke, Yanlong Jiang, Tiancheng Jiang, *Analysis on Decision Dilemma of Dispatch Workers' Claim of "Equal Pay for Equal Work"*, China Labor, 2011, No.12, p. 19.

[27] *Labor Contract Law,* Article 57.

agencies to register with a labor administration agency and prior license was not required.

Second, the revision put more stress on the principle of equal pay for equal work. The provision stated: "labor remuneration specified in the labor contract between the labor dispatch agency and the dispatched worker and the dispatch agreement between the labor dispatch agency and the host company of the dispatched workers should be in compliance with the principle of equal pay for equal work."[28]

Third, the revision imposed further restrictions on the scope of work eligible for labor dispatching. The revision stipulated that labor dispatching could only be used as a supplementary form of employment relationship, applicable to only those job positions that are temporary, auxiliary, and substitutions. A position is "temporary" if the duration is less than six months; it is "auxiliary" if the position is to provide business service support for main business job positions; and it is a "substitution" when the person who ordinarily occupies the post is on temporary leave either to attend professional training or for other causes. The revision provides that the number of dispatched workers must be subject to tight control and shall not exceed a certain percentage of any company's total workforce.[29] Later, the Ministry of Human Resources and Social Security capped it at 10 %.[30]

Fourth, the revision provides further clarification on joint liability relations. The revision provided that "in cases where actions of the host company have caused harm to the dispatched worker, the labor dispatch agency and the host company shall have joint and several liabilities."[31]

These revisions took effect in July 2013. Their impact is still hard to evaluate. But it is doubtful that the revisions have moved us closer to providing full protection for dispatched workers.

First, although an administrative license is required to operate a labor dispatch business, which provides some assurance that these companies must meet certain requirements at the outset, regular and continuous supervision is still important. But the revisions did not provide a clear provision on the daily monitoring of these agencies. Fortunately, the *Implementation Measures of Administrative License for Labor Dispatching*, effective July 1, 2013, stipulated that labor dispatch agencies have a duty to report while the license issuing agencies have the duty to verify and supervise.[32] These measures go some way toward mitigating the deficiencies in the Labor Contract Law.

---

[28] *Labor Contract Law,* Article 63.

[29] *Labor Contract Law,* Article 66.

[30] *Interim Provisions on Labor Dispatch of 2014,* Article 4.

[31] *Labor Contract Law,* Article 92.

[32] Article 22 of the *Implementation Measures of Labor Dispatch Administrative License* stipulates: A labor dispatch agency shall submit a report to the license issuing agency by March 31 each year regarding its labor dispatch operation of the previous year. The following items must be reported truthfully:

1. business operation and finance audit report of the previous year;
2. number of dispatched workers, labor contracts entered, and how many joined trade unions;

Second, although a premium has been placed on the principle of equal pay for equal work, realizing this is still very difficult, especially under the current situation where anti-discrimination legislation is underdeveloped and enforcement weak.

Third, although the revisions clarified the scope of labor dispatching, it still falls short on giving clear definitions of concepts such as "temporary," "auxiliary," and "substitution". And the requirement that dispatched workers should make up no more than 10 % of any employer's total workforce does not consider the different needs of different enterprises. Therefore, this requirement may place extra burden of compliance on some small enterprises.

Fourth, the provisions on joint and several liability are still problematic. Joint and several liability is conducive to lawful operation of labor dispatch agencies and host companies alike as it is meant to protect dispatched workers. However, according to the revision, joint and several liability applies only in situations where actions of the host company have caused harm to the dispatched worker, but not in harm to the dispatched worker was done by the labor dispatch agency. Therefore, if a small labor dispatch agency with limited registered capital has violated the law and done something that caused harm to a dispatch worker, but the labor dispatch agency is unwilling or unable to be held liable, then the host company will not have joint and several liability. This is not beneficial to the protection of the dispatch worker's rights.

6.5 Problems to Be Solved in China's Labor Dispatch System

6.5.1 "Joint Employer" or Not? Ambiguity in the Legal Status of the Host Company

The complexity of legal relationships in labor dispatching lies in the fact that the relationship involves three parties. According to the *Labor Contract Law*, the dispatch agency is the employer of the dispatched worker, a relationship which is quite clear. But there is no consensus on whether the exact nature of the relationship

---

3. wage paid to dispatched workers;
4. purchase of social security insurance and premium payment of dispatched workers;
5. employers of dispatched workers, number of workers to each employer, period of work, and job positions;
6. dispatch agreements signed with employers and fulfillment situation of the agreements;
7. subsidiaries and branches of dispatch agencies. When dispatch agencies set up subsidiaries or branches, a dispatch operation report of the previous year shall be submitted to the administrative agency.

Article 23 stipulates: the license issuing agency should review the annual report submitted by labor dispatch agencies, conduct supervision and enter the results of review and inspection into the enterprise credibility records.

between the host company and the dispatched worker. Specifically, it is neither clear whether the dispatched worker and the host company are related to each other in a labor relationship nor clear whether the host company is a joint employer of the dispatched worker. In General, there are two models in other countries: the "sole employer" and the "joint employer" models. In the "sole employer" model, more commonly used in some European countries, the dispatch agency is considered the only legal employer of the dispatched worker and bears liabilities in that capacity.[33] For instance, in Germany, although dispatched workers provide labor service to clients of the dispatch agency and receive instruction and supervision from the latter, no labor relationship is considered to exist between the two. The dispatched worker has a labor relationship with the dispatch agency only and is regarded an employee of that agency.[34] On a "joint employer" model, there is a "special labor relationship" between the dispatch agency and the dispatched worker, as well as between the host company and the dispatched worker. Both the dispatch agency and its client, the host company, are "joint employers" to the dispatched worker, who will perform the employers' duties such as prescribed in labor laws.[35] The U.S. has adopted the "joint employer" theory in its federal labor laws.[36]

Which model should China adopt, "sole employer" or "joint employer"? Current legal provisions and facts on the ground indicate that dispatch agencies do fulfill such legal duties as recruitment, placement, termination, remuneration disbursement, and social insurance contribution for the dispatched workers. Therefore, there is little doubt that labor dispatch agencies are the "legal employer" of dispatched worker. The issue is whether the client of the dispatch agency, or the host company, is also an "employer". Under Article 62 of the *Labor Contract Law*, the host company should fulfill such duties as providing proper workplace conditions and protections, overtime pay, bonuses, relevant benefits, and necessary training. In addition, since most if not all host companies also provide instruction and management on a regular basis, and dispatched workers are subject to their control, these companies do in fact fulfills certain duties of the employer. For these reasons, the host company should also be regarded as an "employer" of the dispatched worker.

As a matter of fact, the instruction, management, and control of the dispatched worker by the dispatch agency and the host company cannot be completely separated. Rather, their management roles manifest themselves in different aspects and stages of the dispatch relationship. For instance, the dispatch agency exercises management mainly over recruitment, contract signing, remuneration, social security payment, and termination, whereas the host company mainly exercises management

[33] Rongfang Zhang, *On the Model of China's Legal Restrictions of Labor Dispatch*, Law Review, 2009, No.6, p. 56.

[34] Heping Cai, *The Employee Transfer Law in Germany and Its Development,* in Changzheng Zhou (ed.), The Development of Labor Dispatch and Legal Regulation, China Labor and Social Security Press, 2007, p. 89.

[35] Baohua Dong, *Legal Reflection on Labor Dispatch,* China Labor, 2005, No.6, p. 11.

[36] Zengyi Xie, *Labor Dispatch Laws and Regulations of the United States and Ideas for China's Labor Dispatch Legislation*, Comparative Law Study, 2007, No. 6, p. 110.

over labor contract compliance, daily monitoring, overtime pay, safety and health. The two employers also make some decisions jointly. According to the Article 59 of the *Labor Contract Law*, the dispatch agreement between the labor dispatch agency and the host company also reflects the common will of both parties. Therefore, based on the dispatched worker's relationships with the dispatch agency and the host company respectively, and the joint action of the dispatch agency and the host company, the two constitute the "joint employers" of the dispatched worker.

It's worth pointing out that although the legal relationship is simpler in the "sole employer" model, which is free of some legal complexities and is the model adopted by some European countries, its suitability depends on the context and is based on certain premises. First, in some European countries, while dispatched workers have only temporary or otherwise short-term assignments at any host company, their relationship with the dispatch agency is relatively stable and steady.[37] Therefore, laying the duties associated with an employer at the feet of dispatch agencies not only makes practical sense but is also beneficial to the dispatched worker. Moreover, this model requires strict and effective regulation of dispatch agencies. They must abide by the law and be capable of taking on accountability and liability. This places a high demand on the industry in terms of the general legislative environment, the credibility of dispatch agencies and their level of compliance with the law. Obviously, current conditions in China are not yet ripe for the adoption of this model.

The purpose of identifying as "joint employers" the dispatch agency and the host company is to establish the legal basis for defining their duties and liabilities, especially in the following two aspects:

First, the "joint employer" framework lays down the foundation for the right to equal pay for equal work. This principle requires the employer to provide equal treatment for dispatched workers and regular, i.e., directly hired employees. Usually, this principle is applicable to people working for the same employer and incomparable positions.[38] Therefore, the person claiming this right must have a labor relationship with the employer.[39] If no such relationship exists between the dispatched worker and the host company, and the dispatched worker is not regarded as an employee in that company, it will be very difficult for them to press this claim against that company. Therefore, clearing recognizing the relationship between a host company and dispatched workers as a labor relationship makes it possible for the dispatched worker to claim the right to pay parity with that company.

Second, the "joint employer" framework provides a legal basis for placing the burden of liability on the employer. A provision of the *Labor Contract Law* states that: "in the case that actions by the host company have caused harm to the dispatched worker, the dispatch agency and the host company have joint and several

[37] Rongfang Zhang, *On the Model of China's Legal Restrictions of Labor Dispatch*, Law Review, 2009, No.6, p. 53.

[38] Yanjun Feng, *Doubts and Reflections on the Principle of Equal Pay for Equal Work*, Studies of Law and Commerce, 2011, No. 2, p. 66.

[39] Yongqian Tu, *Causes of Labor Dispatch Abuse and Legal Restrictions*, Forum of Political Science and Law, 2013, No.1, p. 181.

liabilities." Some scholars argue that this joint and several liability provision lacks theoretical basis.[40] Whether there should be a joint and several liability depends on whether a labor relationship obtains among the dispatched worker, the dispatch agency, and the host company. As earlier analysis indicates, since they are "joint employers," both the dispatch agency and the host company should take joint and several liabilities. This will encourage the host company to be more cautious in the use of dispatched workers, and thereby help reduce abuse.

6.5.2 *Improving Enforcement Mechanisms*

Article 63 of the revised *Labor Contract Law* clarified that the responsibility for ensuring that dispatched workers' right to equal pay for equal work is enforced falls upon the host company, something that was unclear in the earlier version of the law. Equality in pay for the dispatched workers is measured in reference to the remuneration rate for host company's regular employees. The revised law stressed that both the host employer and the labor dispatch agency have joint duty to enforce equal pay for equal work.[41] These clarifications add legal teeth to the principle of equal pay for equal work. But still, the provisions about host companies' legal duty are insufficient for guaranteeing that dispatched workers' right to equal pay for equal work is actually realized. In the future, the principle of "equal pay for equal work" should be integrated into the framework of anti-discrimination laws, and enforced via an anti-discrimination mechanism. Moreover, equality for dispatched workers should not be limited to remuneration, but should also include overtime pay, break, holiday and vacation leave, and other benefits.[42] Chinese legislators could consider drawing on from the European Union's Council Directive No. 2008/104 on *Temporary Agency Work* and require that employers treat dispatched workers and their regular employees equally.[43] Only sound anti-discrimination legislation with an effective enforcement mechanism can make equal pay for equal work a reality for dispatched workers.

[40] Jia Lin, Wei Fan, *Analysis of China's Legal Restrictions on Labor Dispatch,* Academic Journal of Renmin University of China, 2011, No.6, p. 76.

[41] One Section was added to Article 63 of the revised *Labor Contract Law*: "The labor remuneration specified in the labor contract entered between the labor dispatch agency and the dispatched worker, and the dispatch agreement entered with the employer must be in compliance with the previous prevision hereof".

[42] For instance, the European Council Directive clearly stipulates that dispatched workers and regular workers should enjoy equal treatment in work hours, overtime, rest, holidays, night shift, vacation, and wages. See, Council Directive No. 2008/104, Article 3.

[43] Article 5, Council Directive No. 2008/104 on Temporary Agency Work.

Chapter 7
Termination of Labor Contracts

The termination of labor contracts is an important issue in labor law and disputes over termination account for a large percentage of the cases handled by arbitration agencies and the courts. This is because employees usually do not try to challenge their employers when they are still employed. Often it is only when a contract is about to be terminated or when an employee is dismissed will grievances be aired and demands pressed. The main issues in the termination of labor contracts include the legitimacy of the grounds for termination, related compensation, and liabilities for wrongful termination, and so on.

7.1 Legitimate Grounds for Dismissals Under Chinese Law

Like in many European countries, Chinese law also requires employers to have legitimate grounds for dismissing an employee. A list of such grounds is given in Articles 39–41 of China's *Labor Contract Law*. They include: (1) misconduct; (2) illness or non-work related injuries; (3) incompetency; (4) obtainment of circumstances that render honoring the contract unfeasible; and (5) economic layoffs. More specifically, an employee can be dismissed on the following grounds:

First, the employee has engaged in some kind of misconduct.

Under Article 39 of the *Labor Contract Law*, the employer can terminate a labor contract when an employee has engaged in any of the following types of misconduct:

1. "Serious violation of the workplace rule." The law allows only "serious" violations to constitute legitimate grounds for dismissal. "Minor" violations do not count. But there are no clear criteria for determining what is "serious" and in the practice it is decided on a case-by-case basis.
2. "Serious dereliction of duty, acts of malfeasance that resulted in significant damage to the employer." The law allows only "serious" dereliction of duty and acts

Z. Xie, *Labor Law in China*, Research Series on the Chinese Dream and China's Development Path, DOI 10.1007/978-3-662-46929-3_7

of malfeasance that have resulted in "significant" damages to constitute legitimate grounds for dismissal.

3. "The employee is concurrently in a labor relationship with another employer, which has had adverse impact on their ability to perform their job duties adequately, and the employee refuses to change despite warning from the employer." This provision applies in two kinds of situation: first, when the employee's moonlighting has seriously affected their job performance for the primary employer. For instance, this can happen when the second job leaves an employee exhausted, such that their performance at their primary job is compromised. When this happens, the employer can dismiss the employee. Second, when an employee engages in a part-time job despite the employer's objections, the employer can dismiss him/her on this ground. In the latter case, the employer is given the full power to decide whether the employee can moonlight, which may not be reasonable.
4. "When an employee makes the other party either formulate a labor contract or makes changes to an existing one through deception, coercion, manipulation or otherwise by taking unfair advantages," the labor contract is invalid, and the employer has no obligation to abide by it.
5. When "an employee is a subject of criminal responsibility," an indication of serious misconduct, dismissal is justified.

In these cases, the employer can directly notify the employee of the termination of contract without prior notice. According to these statutory provisions, the substantive requirements for legitimate grounds for termination by the employer are relatively stringent. An employee's misconduct has to be "serious" to warrant dismissal; minor misconduct does not.

Second, an employee suffers from certain illnesses or has sustained non-work related injuries.

According to the law, the employee can be dismissed when, "the employee cannot return to work in either their old position or a new one after the prescribed treatment period for an illness or non-work related injuries."[1] Under this provision, an employer cannot dismiss an employee altogether if their physical conditions prevent them from performing their job duties in the current position. The employer must arrange another position for the employee. If the employee cannot perform adequately in that position either, then they can be dismissed. Also, the employer must give a 30-day written notice to the employee or pay the employee an additional one-month wage before the contract can be terminated.

Third, the employee is incompetent.

According to the law, "when an employee is incompetent and is incapable of performing their job adequately, and shows no improvement after receiving training or trying different positions,"[2] the employer can terminate the contract. The employer must first provide training or adjust the job position for an incompetent employee.

[1] *Labor Contract Law,* Article 40, Sec. 1.

[2] *Labor Contract Law,* Article 40, Sec. 2.

If thereafter the employee is still incompetent, then they can be dismissed. Also, the employer must give a 30-day written notice to the employee or pay the employee an additional one-month wage before the contract can be terminated.

The above-mentioned provisions show that when contracts need to be terminated due to an employee's personal reasons, such as health or capability, the employer must first try to make adjustments to that person's job duties or to provide training so as to help correct the situation. This shows that legislators want to make sure that dismissal is the last resort for an employee, one that is considered only after all ways to salvage the situation have been exhausted. Therefore, by making it difficult for the employer to terminate a labor contract, the law offers employee relatively strong protection.

Four, honoring the contract has been rendered infeasible by non-personal or external reasons.

The law provides that "when major changes to those non-personal or external conditions that held when labor contract was signed have taken place, such as to render honoring the original contract infeasible, and negotiations between the employer and employee regarding modifying the original contract results in no agreement," the employee can be dismissed. "Non-personal or external conditions" refers to those conditions that are necessary for performing the original labor contract. When changes to these conditions due to force majeure e.g., natural conditions, corporate relocation, merger, and corporate asset transfer, or other circumstantial changes, render performance of the contract – in part or whole – infeasible, the employee can be dismissed.[3] But these changes must be "major," and the employer's attempt to negotiate a modified contract with the employee must have failed for the dismissal to be justified. Also, the employer must give a 30-day advanced written notice to the employee or pay the employee an additional one-month wage before termination of the contract.[4] Here again the law gives strong protection for the employee by making dismissal the last resort.

Five, dismissal for redundancy.

Like those in many other countries, Chinese laws also allow enterprises to lay off substantial numbers of employees when they experience business difficulties or are making major operational adjustments. According to the *Labor Contract Law*, redundancy dismissal is allowed under any of the following conditions: (1) corporate restructuring enacted in compliance with the *Enterprise Bankruptcy Law*; (2) serious production and operation difficulties; (3) modifications to the original contracts following transformation, major technical innovation, or adjustments to business model have not fully eliminated redundancy; (4) major changes have taken place to those non-personal or external conditions that held when labor contract was signed such as to render honoring the original contract infeasible.[5] If any of the above conditions is satisfied and the number of employees to be laid off either

---

[3] Chunying Xin (ed.), *Interpretation of the Labor Contract Law of the People's Republic of China*, Law Press, 2007, p. 143.

[4] *Labor Contract Law*, Article 40, Sec. 3.

[5] *Labor Contract Law*, Article 41.

exceeds 20, or account for more than 10 % of the total workforce, the employer can proceed with the dismissal, provided they have submitted an explanation of the situation to either the trade union or all employees 30 days in advance, solicited feedback therefrom, and reported the laid-off proposal to the relevant labor administrative agency. Redundancy dismissal procedure is more complicated compared to that for dismissing an individual employee. Specifically, in the former, but not the latter case, an explanation must be submitted to the trade union or all employees, their voices must be heard, and the lay-off proposal must be reported to the labor administrative agency, even though its approval is not needed. The main purpose of the reporting requirement is to make sure the agency is informed and can supervise the employer over their compliance with all due legal procedures and monitor the social effects that the layoff might have.

The law also provides that all employees are not treated the same in a redundancy dismissal and the employer must try to spare the job of some employees, including (1) those who are on long fixed-term labor contracts; (2) those who have a non-fixed-term contract with the employer; and (3) those who are the sole breadwinner in their family, and who have elderly and/or minor dependents.[6] As such, this provision functions as a strong social policy.

In short, legitimate grounds for dismissals fall into three categories: (1) personal reasons related to the employee, such as misconduct, poor health condition, and incompetency; (2) business-related economic reasons; and (3) non-personal and external reasons related to the conditions of the employer.

7.2 Legitimate Grounds for Dismissal in Some Other Countries

Dismissal Rule is a core issue in labor law. Many countries have established rules and regulations for dismissal through statues and case law. Studying them can help China improve its legal system governing dismissal.

7.2.1 The U.K.

In the U.K., both common law and statute law may apply to rescinding or terminating labor contracts. In common law, the basic principles pertaining to contracts are adopted that treat the employer and employee as equal parties. But apart from requiring prior notice, the law provides no further protective measure for the employee, and the employer can dismiss the employee without justification. For purposes of promoting employment security and enhancing protection for the

[6] *Labor Contract Law,* Article 41.

employee, statutes have been adopted in the U.K. to make up for the deficiencies in common law. Statutes require dismissal to be justifiable. According to the 1996 *Employment Rights Act,* legitimate grounds for dismissal include the following: (1) An employee is either unable to fulfill their job duties, i.e., is unable to do their job at all or to reach an acceptable standard in their job performance due to illness or accident, or is lacking in qualification, such as diploma, degree, or other professional or technical credential related to the job; (2) An employee has engaged in misconduct such as serious absenteeism or lateness, disloyalty, refusal to obey legitimate and reasonable employer instructions, dishonesty, violence, or other disorderly conduct; (3) An employee is subject to redundancy dismissals due to business-related economic reasons; (4) An employee is unable to continue working in a job due to legal prohibitions. For instance, when an employee whose primary or sole responsibility is to drive a vehicle is no longer qualified to drive, the employee can be legitimately dismissed; (5) When other substantive reasons apply, including "business necessity" and "third-party pressure."[7]

7.2.2 Germany

Rescission and termination of labor contracts is a very complicated issue in Germany. The main governing laws are the *Civil Codes* and the 1969 *Protection Against Unfair Dismissal Act.* According to the *Act*, an employee can only be dismissed for legitimate reasons, which fall into three categories: an employee's personal reasons; an employee's conduct; and apparently employer-related business reasons. Unless it is for one of the above-mentioned reasons, a dismissal will be deemed invalid for being "socially unjustified."[8]

(1) Personal reasons that can constitute legitimate ground for dismissal mainly include illnesses that leave an employee unable to work for extended periods of time. But case law indicates that dismissal can only be a last resort when it comes to employees with illnesses. If the business is large enough, and the problem of an employee's temporary absence due to illness can be solved in other ways, courts usually do not support dismissal.[9] (2) In the category of personal conduct, dismissal is justified when the employee has breached their contractual duties.[10] (3) Business-related grounds of dismissal mainly include economic crisis and such economic measures taken by the employer as adoption of new technology. The burden of proof is on the employer to show that retaining the employee is economically

[7] *Employment Rights Act 1998*. See also, Deborah J Lockton, Employment Law, 5th Edition, Palgrave Macmillan, 2006, pp. 292–308.

[8] *Protection Against Unfair Dismissal Act* (2001), §1.

[9] Blanpain, Bison-Rapp, Corbett, Josephs, and Zimmer, *The Global Workplace: International and Comparative Employment Law-Cases and Materials*, Cambridge University Press, 2007, p. 400.

[10] Stefan Lingemann, Robert von Steinau-Steinruck and Anja Mengel, *Employment and Labor Law in Germany*, Verlag C.H. Beck, 2003, p. 28.

unreasonable. For instance, this happens when the introduction of new work or production methods, factory closing, outsourcing, factory relocation, and so forth results in the need to streamline the workforce. If some of the current employees can be placed in other vacant positions, the employer has a duty to do so instead of laying them off, and must provide these employees with the necessary education and training opportunities.[11] These provisions show that, in Germany, legitimate grounds of dismissal are subject to stringent requirement.

7.2.3 *France*

In France, the *Labor Code* recognizes the employer's right to dismiss the employee, but there must be a legitimate reason, i.e. a "real and serious reason." When dismissing an employee, the employer has the burden of proof to establish a justification that is based on either personal reasons or economic reasons. The French *Labor Code* does not specify the allowable types of "personal reasons," but case law indicates that the following are acceptable: (1) professional incompetence; (2) poor job performance, including the failure to accomplish work assignment or reach sales targets; (3) professional misconduct; (4) the employer's having lost confidence in the employee; or (5) sexual harassment, and so on. In addition to these substantive reasons, French law also has strict procedural requirements for dismissal.[12] The employer can also dismiss the employee for "economic reasons." These reasons include company restructuring that has affected the employee's job position, or economic difficulties or technical changes that have led to a substantial change to the terms of the labor contract. These reasons have nothing to do with the employee's own conduct.[13]

7.2.4 *Japan*

There are no provisions governing specific grounds for dismissal in Japanese statutes. Article 18 Section 2 of the *Labor Standards Law* stipulates that "if the dismissal lacks objective reasonable justification and is not proper under overall social

---

[11] Stefan Lingemann, Robert von Steinau-Steinruck and Anja Mengel, *Employment and Labor Law in Germany*, Verlag C.H. Beck, 2003, p. 31.

[12] Blanpain, Bison-Rapp, Corbett, Josephs, and Zimmer, *The Global Workplace: International and Comparative Employment Law-Cases and Materials,* Cambridge University Press, 2007, pp. 437–439.

[13] Blanpain, Bison-Rapp, Corbett, Josephs, and Zimmer, *The Global Workplace: International and Comparative Employment Law-Cases and Materials*, Cambridge University Press, 2007, pp. 441–442.

conditions, the dismissal shall be regarded an abuse of power and deemed invalid."[14] Article 16 of the *Labor Contract Law* enacted in 2007 in Japan has a similar provision,[15] but it too did not specify allowable grounds for dismissal.

For a long time in Japan, legitimate reasons for dismissal were determined on the basis of case law. Over the years courts in Japan have learned through practice that it is necessary to impose restrictions on employers in regard to dismissal. For this purpose, the court applies "the abuse of right" provision in the civil code and holds that if the dismissal is objectively unreasonable or socially unacceptable, then the dismissal shall constitute an abuse of right. Thus, although there are no statutory provisions specifying types of permissible ground for dismissal, in reality, dismissals must be based on legitimate reasons to be supported by the court.[16] Since the beginning of the twenty-first century, courts have eased some of the overly strict requirements for dismissal and relaxed conditions for economic layoffs.[17]

7.2.5 The U.S.

"Employment at will" has been the fundamental principle in U.S. employment law. Under this principle, unless the contract has a fixed-term, the employer can dismiss an employee for any reason or no reason at all. This was the unshakable core principle of U.S. employment law since it was established in 1877, until the end of the nineteenth century. The principle went almost unchallenged in the first half of the twentieth century, and two restrictions were later added. One was due to the adoption of the *National Labor Relations Act* in 1935, which gave employees the right to organize and participate in trade unions and collective bargaining. And many collective bargaining agreements prohibited employers from dismissing an employee without a "legitimate reason." Another was based on rules about state and local government employees, which give them special legal protections and proscribe their willful dismissal.[18] But even with these and other restrictions introduced since 1930s, "employment at will" remains the fundamental principle in U.S. employment law. Exceptions to the norm are few and far between, and subject to strict scrutiny. This is a significant difference between employment law in the U.S. and in many countries, especially European countries.

The above discussion shows that, apart from the U.S., European and continental law countries have basically the same requirements for dismissal. Legitimate

[14] Japan *Labor Standards Law,* revised 2004, effective 2005, English version, Article 18(2).

[15] Japan *Labor Contract Law*, 2007, English version, Article 16, Supplementary Article 2.

[16] Takashi Araki, *Labor and Employment Law in Japan*, the Japan Institute of Labor, 2002, pp. 23–24.

[17] Takashi Araki, *Labor and Employment Law in Japan*, the Japan Institute of Labor, 2002, pp. 25–26.

[18] Mark A. Rothstein, Charles B. Craver, Elinor P. Schroeder, Elaine W. Shoben, *Employment Law*, West, 2005, pp. 746–747.

reasons basically fall into two categories: personal reasons related to the employee's own physical and health conditions, incompetence, and misconduct, and employer's business difficulties and major adjustments. When either one of these two types reasons holds, the dismissal is legal. In Japan, the principle of justified dismissal is established through case law. And in the U.S., under the free market system, in general, no legitimate reason is required for dismissal. In China, dismissal rules are similar to those in European countries, requiring dismissals to be based on legitimate grounds. Employers are subject to strict rules about dismissal, which tend to favor the employee in dismissal cases. This means China's labor laws are strongly protective toward workers.

7.3 Employer Duty to Provide Severance Allowance

When an employee is dismissed for legitimate reasons, the dismissed employee usually can receive some form of compensation, which is referred to as "severance allowance" by the International Labor Organization (ILO), as "redundancy pay" in the U.K., and as "economic compensation" in China. There are some controversies regarding the nature and applicable scope of severance allowance.

According to the ILO's *Convention concerning Termination of Employment at the Initiative of the Employer* of 1982 (No. 158), a worker whose employment has been terminated shall be entitled to a severance allowance or other separation benefits, the amount of which shall be based *inter alia* on length of service and the level of wages, and paid directly by the employer or by a fund constituted by employers' contributions. When a worker's employment is terminated for serious misconduct, the employer does not need to pay a severance allowance or other separation benefits.[19] Although ILO's convention provides detailed rules on this issue, provisions regarding severance allowance vary a great deal among different countries.

7.3.1 Severance Allowance Provisions in Select Countries

In the U.K., redundancy pay by the employer is only required for dismissals on the ground of economic redundancy. The amount is based on the employee's age during employment and length of service. For those employees under the age of 22 during their tenure at the company, they are paid at the rate of half a week's wage for each year with the company, for those between the ages of 22 and 41, the rate is a full week's wage for each year at the company, and those over the age of 41, the rate is one and a half week's wage for each year with the company. But the total amount shall not exceed the legal maximum wage, and the number of years to be counted

[19] Convention Concerning Termination of Employment at the Initiative of the Employer (Termination of Employment Convention, 1982), Article 12 (1),(3).

for this purpose is capped at 20.[20] An employee is not entitled to redundancy pay if guilty of misconduct.[21]

In France, if an employee has worked for the employer for at least one year and the employment has been terminated for personal or economic reasons, the employee is entitled to a severance allowance except in cases of gross negligence or deliberate misconduct. The amount shall be based on the employee's length of service, the labor contract, or the collective agreement. The law only stipulates the minimum amount for the severance allowance, which is 10 % of the monthly wage for each year of employment. According to the standard set by law, employees who have been with the employer for ten years are eligible for severance allowance in the amount of one full month's wage.[22] This shows that in France, while dismissal for either personal or economic reasons entitles the dismissed to severance allowance, the amount is low.

In Germany, the requirements for legitimate termination are stringent, and if the court supports the employer's reason for dismissal, then no severance allowance needs to be paid, even for economic layoffs. Only when an employee is let go without legitimate reasons will the employer execute the termination by giving severance pay. The amount will be calculated at the rate of half a month's wage for each year with the employer, and for regular employees the amount shall not exceed 12 months' wage.[23]

In the U.S., under the principle of employment at will, the employer can dismiss the employee without a legitimate reason. And neither statutes nor case law require of the employer to pay severance allowance.

In Japan, although there are statutory provisions and case law for termination and layoffs, there is no severance allowance provision in statutes. This is similar to statutory laws in Germany.

We can conclude, therefore, that except for the US, most other countries have similar basic requirements for legitimate grounds for dismissal. However, provisions for severance allowance tend to vary greatly from country to country.

7.3.2 Severance Allowance Under Chinese Law

According to Article 46 of the *Labor Contract Law,* economic compensation shall be paid to a dismissed employee in the following situations: (1) the employee's contract is terminated due to an employer's illegal conduct; (2) the contract is terminated at the employer's initiative and an agreement is reached between the

[20] Deborah J Lockton, *Employment Law*, 5th Edition, Palgrave Macmillan, 2006, pp. 348, 365.

[21] *Employment Rights Act* 140(1).

[22] Aiqing Zheng, *General Introduction on French Labor Contract Law,* Guangming Daily Press, 2010, p. 165.

[23] Blanpain, Bison-Rapp, Corbett, Josephs, and Zimmer, *The Global Workplace: International and Comparative Employment Law-Cases and Materials*, Cambridge University Press, 2007, p. 401.

parties; (3) the contract is terminated by the employer due to the employee's health conditions or poor job performance; (4) the contract is terminated due to reasons related to the employer which render honoring the contract infeasible; (5) economic layoffs due to the employer's business performance; (6) expiration of a fixed-term labor contract; (7) the employer has declared bankruptcy, had its business license cancelled, been ordered to close, or dissolved on its own.

Also, according to Article 47 of the *Labor Contract Law,* the compensation rate shall be one-month's wage for each year of employment with the company. If the employee's monthly wage (i.e. the average wage during the 12 months immediately prior to termination) is more than three times the local average wage from the previous year, they will be paid based on three times the average local wage and the number of years to be counted will be capped at 12.[24] If the employee's wage does not exceed three times the local average wage, then there shall be no upper limit for economic compensation. Therefore, when compared with the countries mentioned above, China is more generous in regard both to the scope of eligibility for economic compensation for the dismissed and to the legally required amount to be paid. This may constitute a burden for employers.

7.3.3 Reasons for the Differences of the Rules in Different Countries and Regions

Even though the ILO has adopted relevant conventions and recommendations, large disparities in severance allowance standards persist among different countries, and it is worth considering the reasons for this. Some of them are as follows:

First, severance allowance and other forms of benefits are sometimes intersubstitutable. Although there are different theories regarding the nature of severance allowance among different countries, a basic consensus is that an important function of severance allowance is to provide the temporarily unemployed compensation or relief as a form of protection. Therefore, unemployment and other forms of welfare benefits may have the same or similar functions as severance allowance. This is typically reflected in the 1982 ILO's *Convention Concerning Termination of Employment at the Initiative of the Employer* of 1982 (No. 158). The *Convention* stipulates that a worker whose employment has been terminated shall be entitled to: (1) severance allowance or other separation benefits; (2) benefits from unemployment insurance or assistance or other forms of social security, or (3) a combination of such allowance and benefits.[25] Thus, when a labor contract is revoked or terminated, i.e., when a worker becomes unemployed, severance allowance and other forms of social security or social relief programs (typically unemployment benefits) can substitute for each other to offer relief for the unemployed. Therefore, in countries and

[24] *Labor Contract Law,* Article 47.

[25] Convention Concerning Termination of Employment at the Initiative of the Employer (Termination of Employment Convention, 1982), Article 12.

regions where there is no severance allowance, other unemployment benefits or payment from social security programs can play the same or similar role.

Second, difference among countries in terms of collective bargaining rules and due process requirements in the law also helps explain some of the differences in legal rules about severance allowance. Many countries have strict legal procedural requirements for talks and negotiations, especially in large-scale layoffs. These requirements provide sound procedural safeguards that enable negotiation between the employer and employee regarding severance allowance. In these negotiations, in the absence of statutory provisions, the trade union or workers' representatives can demand severance allowance or other benefits as compensation for the dismissed.

Third, different forms of employment also contribute to differences in rules about severance allowance. The ILO's *Convention Concerning Termination of Employment at the Initiative of the Employer* of 1982 (No. 158) allows member states to make flexible dismissal arrangements for special forms of employment. For instance, the *Convention* states that it applies to all branches of economic activity and to all employed persons. But a member may exclude the following categories of employed persons when applying all or some of the provisions of the *Convention*: (1) workers engaged under a contract of employment for a specified period of time or a specified task; (2) workers serving a period of probation or a qualifying period of employment, determined in advance and of reasonable duration; (3) workers engaged on a casual basis for a short period.[26] Therefore, countries shall make special arrangements for special forms of employment including employees with fixed-term contracts. The arrangements for fixed-term and non-fixed-term contacts are naturally different. Different forms of employment in different countries will lead to differences in rules about severance pay.

Fourth, the inherent flexibility in rules about severance allowance is another reason for the variations. Since severance allowance primarily applies in situations where neither the employer nor the employee is at fault, rules about it mainly reflects the social policies of different countries and thus shows great flexibility. Neither the employer nor the employee is at fault when termination of employment is due to either ill health or incompetence on the part of the employee, or facts about the employer that make it infeasible to execute the contract. Under such circumstances, strong policy considerations guide rules about severance allowance. This makes it difficult to have a uniform system and set of standards.

In short, the scope of severance allowance is relatively broad in China and the rate of it is higher than in most other countries. Since China's unemployment insurance and relief systems are not yet well-developed, and the role of trade unions and collective bargaining is not strong, higher statutory rate of severance allowance can make up for deficiencies in other aspects of the law and its implementation, and are therefore reasonable.

[26] Convention Concerning Termination of Employment at the Initiative of the Employer (Termination of Employment Convention, 1982), Article 2 (b),(c).

7.3.4 The Nature and Purpose of Severance Allowance

Scholars have varied views regarding the nature of severance allowance. Some hold that they are compensation for the worker whose employment contract is terminated by the employer and its scope and standard should be determined by the extent of labor protection of each country.[27] Others hold that, employers' legal right to terminate labor contract allows them to diffuse the risk of running a business operations by shifting some of it to the worker. As such, severance allowance could be regarded as fair burden sharing or risk distribution between the employer and the employee.[28]

In the U.K., severance allowance is provided for by statute and some British scholars have studied the nature of the redundancy pay or severance allowance. According to the British scholar Deborah J. Lockton, this provision by legislation indicates that the purpose of severance allowance or redundancy pay is not to alleviate the consequences of unemployment for the worker, but to recognize the stakes and interests of the employee in the job. Therefore, even if the employee finds another job immediately after the dismissal, the employee is still entitled to the redundancy pay. And the longer the length of service, the bigger the stake; therefore, the size of the redundancy pay should be positively correlated with age and length of service.[29] Professor Lockton believes that the redundancy pay is more a form of compensation for the lost job than unemployment protection. Two other British labor law scholars, Professor Simon Deakin and Professor Gillian Morris, hold that the purpose of the redundancy pay is to help the employee while they look for another job, therefore, those who have reached retirement age should not be entitled to redundancy pay.[30]

Based on statutory provisions and studies of various countries, the nature and function of severance allowance can be summarized as follows:

First, the primary purpose of the severance allowance is to compensate an individual who lost their job due to dismissal for their economic loss. From a legal perspective, the basic value of employment is that it allows the employee to earn a wage and other social benefits as property income. When the employee is fired for reasons related to business performance, or other factors not due to the employee's own fault, and the dismissal is lawful, the employee is deprived of interests derivable from working. Such interests not only include wages and benefits but also the accumulated skills and social reputation during the tenure of their labor service.

[27] Jia Lin, Fei Yang, *Study of Labor Contract Termination Issues Regarding Economic Compensation, Breach of Contract Damages, and Compensation Damages,* in Labor Law Review, Jia Lin (ed.), Renmin University Press, 2005, p. 18.

[28] Yanjun Feng, *The Three Compensations in Labor Contract Termination and the Revision of Labor Law,* in Ten Years' Exploration of Social Justice, Jingyi Ye (ed.), Peking University Press, 2007, pp. 203–204.

[29] Deborah J Lockton, *Employment Law,* 5th Edition, Palgrave Macmillan, 2006, p. 354.

[30] Simon Deakin & Gillian S Morris, *Labor Law* (Fourth Edition), Hart Publishing, Oxford and Portland, Oregon, 2005, pp. 539–540.

Therefore, the employer should compensate the employee for their loss caused by the dismissal. Since the magnitude of this loss is most closely related to the wage level and length of service for the employer, the amount of severance allowance should naturally be linked to these two factors.

Second, severance allowance functions to some extent as a form of social security. An important purpose of severance allowance is to compensate the employee for income loss during unemployment and to help the employee find new employment. This is supported by the ILO's *Convention* provision that severance allowance, unemployment benefits, and other social security programs can substitute for one another. Although some dismissed employees can get unemployment benefits, many cannot, or can get only a limited amount, so severance allowance can offer some measure of protection for the dismissed employee during unemployment.

Third, severance allowance can provide some protection to the employee against the risk of dismissal by imposing some constraints on the employer. When the employer has to pay severance allowance, the cost of dismissal increases. This can encourage the employer to give serious consideration to alternative measures before resting to termination of labor contract. Thus, requirements about severance allowance may help maintain the relationship between the employer and the employee and reduce layoffs and unemployment.

7.4 Employer Liability for Wrongful Dismissal

7.4.1 Liability for Wrongful Dismissal Under Chinese Law

Article 39, 40, and 41 of China's *Labor Contract Law* stipulate that dismissal decisions must be justified; otherwise the employer is liable for wrongful dismissal. Article 87 of the *Labor Contract Law* stipulates that when a labor contract is unlawfully terminated, the amount of damages paid by the employer to the employee shall be two times the standard specified in provision Article 47.[31] In other words, when the grounds are legitimate and the dismissal legal, the rate of severance allowance to be paid will be one-month's wage for each year of service, and when the dismissal lacks justification and is wrongful, the amount of compensation payment

[31] Article 47 of the *Labor Contract Law* stipulates: economic compensation shall be paid based on the length of employment of the employee; one-month wage shall be paid for each year of employment service. If length of service is more than 6 months but less than a year, it shall be treated as one year; if less than 6 months, half a month wage shall be paid as the compensation.

If the employee's wage is three times higher than the local average monthly wage published by the municipal level government of the previous year, economic compensation paid shall be based on three times of the local average monthly wage and the payment period shall not be more than 12 years.

Monthly wage refereed here means the employee's average wage of 12 months prior to termination of the labor contract.

doubles. This "doubling rule" is both simple and easy to use, but these are also its shortcomings, that is, it is overly simplistic and rigid as well as wanting in theoretical support.

First, the rationality of the provision is questionable. In cases of lawful dismissal, the severance allowance that the employer must pay is, in the view of legislator and scholars, a form of compensation for the employee's work-related stakes and interests. The longer the time of employment, the higher the stakes, and the greater should the allowance amount be. By contrast, in cases of wrongful dismissal, the damage represents loss of wage and other income for the balance on the contract after its termination. Therefore, severance allowance paid in cases of lawful dismissal and damages paid in cases of wrongful dismissal have different purposes and are based on different rationales. Simple application of the "doubling rule" is ill-advised.

Second, in many cases, the amount of damages consistent with existing rule will be *prima facie* unfair. While the rules require doubling the payment in cases of wrongful dismissal, the actual amount may be either too high or too low. Take for instance a worker with a five-year fixed-term contract, and who has been wrongfully dismissed after one year of work, according to this rule, this individual is only entitled to payment in the amount of two month's wage (two times of one-month's wage). But this amount is too low since that individual will not be compensated for four years' worth of wage and other losses. Also, the "doubling rule" could give the employer a perverse incentive to dismiss an employee earlier than otherwise, especially if the dismissal may be on dubious ground, since the shorter the worker's tenure, the less will be the required compensation payment.

In other situations, however, the compensation could be unjustifiably high. For example, for a 59-year-old employee who has worked for an employer for 40 years and whose wage is not three times higher than the average local wage, their wrongful dismissal shortly before retirement would, according to this rule, entitle them to damage in the amount of two times 40 months' worth of wage, i.e. 80 months' worth of wages. To receive such a large amount damages one year before retirement in the age of 60 seems unreasonable. These are all examples of loopholes that exist in the current provision.

7.4.2 How to Improve the Rules on Employer's Liability for Wrongful Dismissal

7.4.2.1 Factors to Be Considered For Damages in Wrongful Dismissal

The employee's loss in a wrongful dismissal is easier to calculate in cases of fixed-term contracts, and much more difficult for cases involving non-fixed-term contracts. This is because the loss to be counted includes not only wages but also other benefits connected with the employee's terms of employment, such as pension, seniority, and even reputation. Also, non-fixed-term contracts are not lifetime contracts, and may be terminated because of the employee's own fault or some other reasons. Therefore, it is difficult to determine the period of time to be counted when calculating losses in wages and other benefits. In addition, the employee may find a similar position soon after termination or be unable to find another job for an extended period of time, so the final amount of losses for the dismissed employee is uncertain. Moreover, the terminated employee may be entitled to unemployment benefits and other benefit income. Therefore, it is almost impossible to ascertain the actual amount of losses that result from a wrongful termination in the case of a non-fixed-term contract and to provide the exact amount of compensation.

This is why in some countries, such as the U.K. and Germany, the main factors to be considered in determining the damages caused by wrongful dismissal are the wage and the duration of tenure. For instance, in the U.K., financial compensation for the employee in unfair dismissal consists of three components: basic awards, compensatory awards, and additional awards. Basic awards, based on age and length of employment, are for the employee's lost job. Compensatory awards are for the employee's loss after termination. Courts will consider the employee's immediate loss of income, future loss of income, additional loss of benefits, cost of looking for a job, loss of pension and labor protection, and the manner of termination. Immediate loss refers to the loss that is incurred between the time of termination and the time of court hearing minus unemployment and other benefits. Loss of future income takes into consideration possible future unemployment period, but the employee has a duty to mitigate the loss. The maximum limit of a compensatory award is 50,000 GBP under the 1999 *Labor Relations Act* and this amount has increased each year.[32] Courts may order the employer to pay an additional award if the employer refuses reinstatement or to re-enter into a contract, if the dismissal is discriminatory, or if employment is terminated for reasons prohibited by law. An additional award may vary, depending on the causes, from 26 to 52 weeks' worth of wage to 104 weeks or even 156 weeks' worth of wage.[33] This shows the punitive nature of additional awards.

Therefore when determining an employer's liability for wrongful dismissal, the following factors should be considered, in accordance with the specific terms of the labor contract: the employee's wage, seniority, allowances, and other fringe benefits, the balance of time on the contract, the employee's age and their prospects for finding similar work, the possible costs to the employee of looking for another job, possible benefits the employee is entitled to during unemployment, whether the employee is at fault, and the severity of the wrongful conduct and whether there has been a violation of public policies. For instance, a termination is obviously illegal if it is in retaliation for the employee's trade union activities or whistle-blowing for the employer's illegal acts. The employer should have greater liability in these cases. Theoretically, comprehensive consideration of all these factors should be given in individual cases. But to determine the amount of required compensation based on these factors is by no means easy.

[32] *Employment Relations Act* 1999, s. 34(4).

[33] Deborah J Lockton, *Employment Law,* 5th Edition, Palgrave Macmillan, 2006, pp. 348–350.

7.4.2.2 Limits of Liability for Wrongful Dismissal

The above analysis shows that it is almost impossible to figure out the exact of actual loss sustained in a wrongful dismissal case. Many countries, such as the U.K., place a ceiling on the amount of compensation. These kinds of limit are reasonable not only because of the difficulty in calculating the actual value of losses but also for the following reasons:

First, a liability limit is helpful for reducing the burden on the employer. After a wrongful dismissal, the employee may have difficulty in finding another job, and may thus incur a great loss. It will be a heavy burden if all losses are borne by the employer. Especially for some small business, large liability may lead to bankruptcy, which not only hurts the employer but may also adversely affect other employees' continued employment. Moreover, usually the employer has enrolled in unemployment insurance as a source of income for the employee when unemployed. Therefore, the employer's liability should be reduced so that they do not have to bear all the losses.

Second, a liability limit can help an employer manage risk and make recruitment plans. Even though termination is usually accompanied by justified reasons in litigation, an adjudicative authority may not accept these reasons, and there is always the risk of losing the case. If the cost of wrongful dismissal is too high, the employer may become excessively cautious in recruiting, which may hamper workforce construction. For example, after the *Labor Contract Law* was adopted some enterprises became more cautious in hiring.[34] Therefore, proper limits on wrongful termination liability will help the employer with risk control and facilitate the growth of the workforce.

Third, a liability limit may help an employee with job search. If the former employee is compensated fully for total loss of wages and other benefits due to premature termination of a non-fixed-term contract, the individual may be insufficiently motivated to look for another job. Therefore, a suitable limit on wrongful dismissal liability is not only feasible but also beneficial.

7.5 Employee-Initiated Termination of Labor Contracts

When an employee can terminate a contract is another important issue in labor law. Under the current *Labor Contract Law*, the employee can terminate a labor contract under the following three circumstances:

[34] For instance, a project group of the Institute of Population and Labor Economics of Chinese Academy of Social Sciences conducted interviews with enterprises in coastal regions. Quite a few of the enterprises expressed concerns about increased difficulty and cost in termination, therefore would be more cautious in hiring. See Fang Cai (ed.), *China Population and Labor Issues Report, No.10*, Social Sciences Academic Press, 2009, pp. 82–103. Although the survey only covered a few enterprises whose understanding of relevant laws might be limited, it did reflect some enterprises' concern of difficulty in termination.

First, an agreement is reached between the employer and the employee regarding the termination.[35] But who was the one who initiated the termination will have implications for details about the severance allowance. If the termination is initiated by the employer, then payment of a severance allowance is mandatory; but if the termination is initiated by the employee, the employee is not entitled to a severance allowance.[36] In the latter case, the employee has resigned of their own volition and there is no liability on the part of the employer. The termination negotiation can be a protracted process and sometimes it is not clear who initiated it. In such situations, the employer's duty of compensation could be uncertain.

Second, resignation by the employee. According to the law, the employee can terminate a labor contract with a 30-day written notice to the employer.[37] So while a resignation need have no cause, the employee has a duty of prior notice and in case of violation of this duty, the employee is liable for the employer's loss.[38] Thus Chinese labor law gives the employee complete freedom of resignation. In some European countries, there are some restrictions on the employee's right to resign, depending on whether the contract is fixed-term or non-fixed-term. In China, as long as the employee fulfills the duty of notice, the employee can resign without giving any reason. Some people are critical of this provision, arguing it gives the employee too much freedom and is unfair to the employer. But from the point of view of freedom of work and prohibition of forced labor, if the employee is not willing to work, it does not seem that the law should be able to force the employee to continue to do so.

Third, the employee can terminate the contract when the employer has violated the law. According to *Labor Contract Law* provisions, the employee can terminate the contract in the following circumstances: (1) the employer fails to provide labor protection or labor conditions per the contract; (2) the employer fails to pay full remuneration in a timely manner; (3) the employer fails to make social insurance payments for the employee according to the law; (4) workplace rules of the employer violate the law and harm the employee's rights; (5) the labor contract has been entered into or modified against the employee's will through fraud, coercion or the taking of unfair advantage of the employee's vulnerability; (6) the contract exempts the employer from statutory responsibilities and excludes the employee's rights; (7) the employer violates mandatory rules required by law and administrative regulations; (8) the employer coerces the employee to work through means of violence, threat, or illegal restriction of personal freedom; (9) the employer illegally commands and orders the employee to engage in risky and dangerous operations which threatens the employee's personal safety.[39]

When the employer has engaged in illegal conduct, it is the employer who has violated the labor contract and harmed the employee's interest, so naturally the

[35] *Labor Contract Law,* Article 36.

[36] *Labor Contract Law,* Article 46.

[37] *Labor Contract Law,* Article 37.

[38] *Labor Contract Law,* Article 90.

[39] *Labor Contract Law,* Article 38.

employee can terminate the contract and is entitled to compensation according to law.[40] But from the above discussion we can conclude that a severance allowance usually applies only to termination because of the employee's own physical conditions, ability and economic reasons related to the employer's condition. In these cases, neither the employer nor the employee is at fault. Resignation of the employee due to an employer's illegal conduct should be regarded as a forced resignation, or a "constructive dismissal" by the employer. In theory, under such circumstance, the employer's liability should be the liability for wrongful dismissal, as opposed to the duty to pay severance allowance in termination on legitimate grounds. Therefore, when the employee's resignation is in response to illegal conduct by the employer, Article 78 (but not Article 46) of the *Labor Contract Law* should apply.

[40] *Labor Contract Law*, Article 46.

Chapter 8
Work-Related Injury Insurance System

8.1 Overview

Work-related injury insurance is a form of social insurance that provides workers medical assistance and economic compensation for injuries caused by work-related accidents or occupational illnesses.

The work-related injury insurance system has the following features. First, the principle of no fault liability applies. A worker is entitled to work-related injury insurance protection as long as the accident or occupational illness is not the result of the worker's deliberate conduct. Whether the employer is at fault does not affect the employee's entitlement to the injury insurance compensation. Second, since the injury is work-related, and the employer is the source of the risk of injury, it is the employer's duty to pay compensation to the injured worker. Therefore, it is not the employee's duty to make payment towards the insurance, but the sole responsibility of the employer. Third, the injury needs to be verified by a special agency with the necessary expertise. Since work-related injury compensation will be drawn from the Work-related Injury Insurance Fund (the "*Fund*"), a special agency is needed to determine whether the injury is in fact work-related and, if so, the appropriate compensation rate. The agency also disburses the compensation payments.

The work-related injury insurance system was established shortly after the founding of the People's Republic of China. The *Trial Regulations of Injury Insurance for Enterprise Employees* promulgated by the Ministry of Labor in August 1996, was China's first attempt at legal codification of matters related to work-related injury insurance. In April 2003, the State Council introduced the *Work-related Injury Insurance Regulations* ("*Regulations*" of 2003), which established a comprehensive set of rules for work-related injuries. The *Social Insurance Law* was enacted in October 2010. Chapter IV of the *Social Insurance Law* was devoted to work-related injury insurance and made improvements to other rules. In December 2010 the State Council issued *The Decision about Revising Work-related*

Z. Xie, *Labor Law in China*, Research Series on the Chinese Dream and China's Development Path, DOI 10.1007/978-3-662-46929-3_8

Injury Insurance Regulations ("*Regulations*" of 2010). The *Social Insurance Law* and the revised *Regulations* represent continued progress in the work-related injury insurance system.

8.2 Scope of the Program and Qualifications for Eligible Injuries

8.2.1 Who Must Offer the Program to Their Employees

Article 2 of the revised *Regulations* of 2010 stated that all enterprises, public institutions, private non-enterprise entities, foundations, law firms, accounting firms, and individually-owned businesses with hired employees should participate in work-related injury insurance and pay the insurance premium for all their employees. Thus, the scope of work-related injury insurance covers almost all employees except for government agencies. The work-related injury regulations are not applicable to civil servants employed by government agencies.

8.2.2 Work-Related Injuries: Definition and Criteria

Work-related injuries are those injuries sustained in work-related accidents or occupational illnesses. Therefore, a basic necessary requirement for work-related injury is that it must be "work-related". The *Social Insurance Law* and the *Regulations* of 2010 do not have clear definitions for "work-related" but instead have adopted a combination of the attribute listing technique and the method of elimination to define the scope of work-related injuries.

In some countries, the key criterion for determining whether an injury is "work-related" is whether it occurred in the "course of employment." For instance, in the U.S., according to most state laws, work-related injuries must meet the following four criteria: (1) it has to be personal injuries, and some states exclude emotional pain and suffering; (2) the injury has to be caused by an accident, as some states exclude chronic injuries other than traumatic accidents; (3) the injury has to arise out of employment, i.e. the cause of the injury must be work-related; (4) the injury has to occur in the course of employment, i.e., at the employer's workplace and during work hours.[1] Along with the development of workers compensation laws in the U.S., the criteria have changed. There has been a tendency to relax the first three conditions.

First, many courts have held that eligible injuries shall include emotional pain and suffering. Second, the definition of "accidents" has been relaxed. At first, only injuries sustained during "unexpected accidents" would count. But increasingly

[1] Steven Willborn, Stewart Schwab, John Burton, Gillian Lester, *Employment Law: Cases and Materials*, LexisNexis, 2007, p. 903.

those sustained during other types of accidents can also count provided they have caused "unexpected results." For example, when a worker for whom heavy lifting is a routine part of the job and not an unexpected accident sustains a back injury at work, the injury can qualify as work-related injury with "unexpected result." Some states have abandoned the "accident" requirement altogether.

Third, the requirement for establishing a casual relationship has been eased. For instance, as case law develops, it no longer requires of the eligible injury to have been "caused" by work activities, and would now count an injury as being "work-related" if work activities have either "contributed to" or "aggravated" it. Take the following example. If an employee suffers from a ruptured disc while trying to lift a heavy object, the employer cannot claim this is not work-related injury on the ground that the employee has a preexisting condition that renders him more susceptible to such injury and a person with sounder physical constitution would not have suffered it trying to do the same thing.[2] With the relaxation of these three requirements, "in the course of employment" has become the primary determining factor for whether an injury qualifies as "work-related" and as such eligible for compensation under the insurance program.

8.2.3 Categories of Work-Related Injuries

In China, according to Article 14 of the *Regulation* of 2003, an injury is to count as work-related injury when any one of the following is true: (1) the injury was sustained during work-related accidents, during work hours and at the workplace; (2) the injury was caused by accidents that took place during preparatory or cleanup work before or after a shift; (3) the injury was unexpected and due to violence the employee was subjected to while performing their job duties during work hours and at the workplace; (4) occupational illnesses; (5) the employee either sustained injury in accidents that took place while they are off-site for work-related reasons or their whereabouts cannot be accounted for altogether; (6) injuries suffered in accidents involving motor vehicles during commute; (7) other circumstances recognized as work-related injuries by law and administrative regulations.

Therefore, in *Regulations* of 2003, the criteria for work injuries make reference to "work" on three dimensions: they have to have taken place during "work hours," they have to have taken place at the "workplace," and they have to be due to "work-related causes," with the last one being the key. Among these seven types of circumstance the first is the most typical; the third is also caused by work-related accidents, but from an external source; the fifth offers an extension of the spatial and temporal scope of eligible work-related accidents. Therefore, for injuries of the first, third and fifth type, it is usually indisputable that they are work-related. For the second type of injuries, that is, those caused by accidents that happen during preparation or cleanup before or after working hours and at the workplace, they may be considered to have

[2] Benjamin W. Wolkinson and Richard N. Block, *Employment Law: The Workplace Rights of Employees and Employers*, Blackwell, 1996, pp. 212–213.

taken place during working hours, and as such treated as workplace injuries. The fourth type of circumstance, occupational illnesses, refers to illnesses employees suffer while engaging in vocational activities or due to contact with such substances as dust, radioactive materials, or other toxic and hazardous materials, according to article 2 of the *Law on Prevention and Treatment of Occupational Illnesses*. This situation satisfies all three work-related conditions in terms of time, place and causes.

Strictly speaking, injuries caused by accidents during commute do not satisfy the "working hours" and "workplace" requirements. But since a commute has certain relevance to work, whether to treat as work-related injuries those sustained during commute is a matter of social policy. For instance, in Japan, before the *Workers' Accident Compensation Insurance Law* was revised in 1973, injuries that occurred during commute were not considered work-related injuries because they did not occur in the course of employment. But since the risk of being injured during commute to or from work had increased, the government deemed it necessary to provide the same protection for those injured during commute as those injured at work. Therefore, injuries sustained during commute were included in the 1973 revised *Workers' Accident Compensation Insurance Law*.[3] In the U.S., there is more emphasis on workplace injuries happening "in the course of employment," so injuries sustained during commute to or from work are usually not recognized as work-related injuries. An employee can make a workers' compensation claim for only those injuries that occur when the employee is physically at the workplace.[4]

The *Regulations* of 2003 limited compensation-eligible injuries during commutes to only those caused by accidents involving "motor vehicles", thereby disqualifying injuries caused by other kinds of accidents. This was deemed unfair to some victims and its reasonableness was questioned. According to article 14 of the revised *Regulations*, in 2010, workplace injuries during commute would include "injuries caused by traffic accidents for which the employee is not primarily responsible, or injuries caused by accidents involving urban mass transit, passenger ferry or train". It is worth recognizing that while the revision expanded the scope of workplace injuries, restricting eligible injuries to only those from "accidents to which the employee is not primarily responsible" seems overly stringent and harsh to the injured employee.

8.2.4 Circumstances Deemed Work Injuries

According to Article 15 of *the Regulations* of 2010, when an employee is in one of the following situations, they are considered to have suffered work-related injury: (1) death caused by sudden illnesses that strike during working hours and at the workplace, or that occurs within 48 hours of the failure of life-saving efforts; (2) injuries sustained while participating in activities, such as disaster relief, whose

[3] Takashi Araki, *Labor and Employment Law in Japan*, the Japan Institute of Labor, 2002, p. 129.

[4] Mark A. Rothstein, Charles B. Craver, Elinor P. Schroeder, Elaine W. Shoben, *Employment Law*, West, 2005, p. 611.

goals are to defend national and/or public interests; (3) an employee suffers from either a relapse of injuries or disabilities sustained during war or military service and for which they have already received pertinent certificates. Obviously, these provisions are meant for policy purposes, and somewhat deviate from the original meaning of work-related injuries.

The first condition listed above, requiring compensation-eligible death to be "caused by sudden illnesses that strike during working hours and at the workplace, or that occurs within 48 hours of the failure of life-saving efforts" is too rigid. In theory, if an employee dies during working hours and at the workplace of a sudden illness or after life-saving efforts fail, whether the death should be considered work-related injury should depend on the exact cause of death. If work has contributed to it either directly or indirectly by affecting the physical condition of the employee in relevant ways, then the death is work-related, and should be recognized as a work-related injury. Otherwise it should not be so treated. For example, in Japan, "Karoshi" (death from over exhaustion due to the sudden occurrence of heart or brain disease) counts as work-related injury. But there must be evidence that the employee had a heavy workload prior to death. For example, an Administrative Guideline issued by the Ministry of Health in Japan in December 2001 stipulated that if an employee had worked more than 100 hours in overtime during the month immediately prior to the occurrence of illness, or on average more than 80 hours a month in overtime during the 6 months immediately prior to the occurrence of illness, the illness shall be presumed to have been caused by work.[5] Therefore, if a death occurs during working hours and at the workplace, its connection with work should be seriously considered. Additionally, limiting compensation eligibility to deaths that occurred "within 48 hours of the failure of live-saving efforts", seems too rigid.

Treating all injuries sustained while am employee is participating in activities, such as disaster relief, whose goals are to defend national and/or public interests can encourage such conduct. However, such conduct typically has little meaningful connection with the employee's regular duties at their current job and the risks are beyond the control of the employer. Also, it is unclear how best to define "activities whose goals are to defend national and/or public interests" and it may include too much, thereby exposing the employer to unnecessary risks. Therefore, although Article 15 of the *Regulations* of 2010 gives strong protection for employees, it is largely based on a deviation from the original meaning of work-related injury, and its appropriateness requires careful consideration.

8.2.5 Ineligible Cases

According to Article 16 of the *Regulations* in 2003, injuries or death that occur in any of the following situations are not work-related injuries: (1) they have been caused by a criminal act or violation of security rules; (2) they are due to

[5] Takashi Araki, *Labor and Employment Law in Japan*, the Japan Institute of Labor, 2002, pp. 126–127.

drunkenness; (3) the injury is self-inflicted or the death a suicide. The 2010 *Social Insurance Law* revised certain provisions of the *Regulations*, and reduced the number of disqualifying situations. There are two main revisions. First, violation of security rule is no longer considered a ground for exclusion. Second, criminal negligence is no longer considered a ground for exclusion. According to Article 37 of the current *Social Insurance Law*, four types of situations disqualify an injury as a work-related: (1) intentional crimes; (2) alcohol or substance abuse; (3) self-inflicted injury or suicide; (4) other circumstances stipulated by law and administrative regulations not to constitute material condition for work-related injuries.

Allowing injuries sustained while an employee is engaging in activities that are in violation of security rules to count as workplace injury is in line with the principle of "no-fault" liability in work-related injury and as such laudable. It is also necessary to make the distinction between criminal negligence and intentional crime, and to include injuries or death caused by criminal negligence as work-related injuries. This is because a no-fault presumption on the part of the injured employee is not made when determining whether an injury counts as work-related. Also, since workplace injury compensation are often very important to the health, life and family of the employee, especially in cases of injuries that lead to disability, it is reasonable to treat injuries or death caused by criminal negligence as work-related and as such eligible for compensation. The revised *Regulations* of 2010 and *Social Insurance Law* are consistent on this point.

Of course there is room for further study and discussion about what the exact scope work-related injuries should be. Currently, injuries caused by drunkenness are not recognized as work-related, but what if drinking is part of a job or otherwise related to work? For instance, if an employee suffers an alcohol-induced injury or death after drinking under pressure or duress from the employer who claims this is necessitated by work, disqualifying such injury or death as work-related does not reasonable. Also, should self-mutilation or suicide be categorically excluded from the scope of work-related injuries? According to case law in the U.S., mental health conditions caused by work-related chronic stress, anxiety or despair may be protected under workers' compensation.[6] In Japan, "overwork suicide" has been a cause for concern in recent years. In the past, most suicide cases, including suicide caused by overwork and depression, were regarded as the employee's voluntary conduct and were ineligible for workers' compensation protection. Several lower courts have overturned such administrative decisions since 1996. These courts have held that since the mental state of the deceased was very unstable, rendering them incapable of resisting the impulse to end one's life, such suicide should not be regarded as voluntary. According to the 1999 *Guidance for Administrative Agencies*, when an employee commits suicide due to work-related stress and mental disorder, the employee's capacity for rational judgment has been severely impaired, and the suicide should be regarded as having work-related causes.[7]

---

[6] 361 Mich. 577, 106 N.W. 2d 105 (1960).

[7] Takashi Araki, *Labor and Employment Law in Japan*, the Japan Institute of Labor, 2002, pp. 126–127.

Therefore, when self-mutilation or suicide is caused by work-related mental distress or a loss of self-control, it should be recognized as work-related injury. Because at this point the employee has lost the ability to control his/her behavior, the act is not entirely voluntary. But, if the suicide or self-mutilation is entirely intentional, it should not be recognized as a work-related injury. Therefore, not all suicide or self-mutilation should be excluded from the scope of work-related injury protection. This is especially important given the recent rise in the incidence of work-related stress mental illness, and self-mutilation or suicides attributable to these causes.

In summary, the basic identifying criteria for work-related injuries are the three conditions related to work, with having "work-related" causes being key among them. Since the concept of "work-related" is elastic, each country would adjust its scope of work-related injuries according to the risks employees face and the country's labor protection policies in general.

8.3 Procedures for Claiming Work-Related Injury Compensation

According to the *Regulations* of 2010, when an employee suffers injuries caused by accidents or has been diagnosed with an occupational illness, the employer should file a compensation application with the labor administrative agency within 30 days of the date of the accident or diagnosis. In cases where the employer does not file the application directly, the injured employee or his or her immediate family or the trade union representing him or her can do so within one year of the accident or diagnosis. If after treatment and stabilization of the condition an injury leads to a disability that compromises the employee's ability to continue to work, an evaluation should be performed to ascertain the employee's suitability for working in the same position.[8] The employee can apply for workplace-related compensation after the verification of work-related injury and the afore-mentioned evaluation have been completed.

The procedure for claiming workers' compensation was overly cumbersome before the 2010 revision of the *Regulations*. The employee had to apply for work-related injury verification with the labor administrative agency and provide proof of a labor relationship with the employer. In many cases, the employer would deny that a labor relationship existed, in which case it is incumbent upon the employee to first request arbitration to establish the existence of such a relationship. The employee may have to go through arbitration and court adjudication, which may take a long time. If the employee or the employee's immediate family or the employer is unsatisfied with the decision on the decision of whether the injury is work-related or not, they can apply for administrative review; and if they are unsatisfied with the result of the administrative review, an administrative lawsuit can be filed according to law.

[8] Evaluation of work ability refers to the determination of degree of work ability impediment and self-care impediment.

Therefore, the employee may need to go through an administrative review and the first and second hearing of administrative litigation just to determine whether the injury is work-related. The whole process can be very time-consuming. And if the employee or the employee's immediate family does not agree with the concerned agency's decisions about injury compensation, they can also apply for administrative review, and if still unsatisfied with the result of that, they can file an administrative lawsuit according to law. Therefore, the employee may need to go through administrative review and the two rounds of administrative litigation hearing just to claim injury compensation, which, again, takes a long time. And if an evaluation for suitability for continued service is involved, its outcome must be decided by a municipal-level committee. The result can be appealed to a provincial-level evaluation committee. Therefore, the evaluation can be a complicated process as well.

This discussion shows that, while the procedure for workers' compensation provides the employee with several channels for remedies it is too cumbersome and involves a large number of agencies. Each of the steps – from establishing a labor relationship to verifying the injury to evaluating the employee for suitability for future service to claiming compensation – calls for a different set of paperwork and filing requirement. All these have made it difficult for the employee to receive compensation in a timely manner.

Three major revisions in the revised *Regulations* of 2010 were meant to help simplify the procedure. First, according to article 20, the revised *Regulations* added one provision for an express option for verifying work-related injury. When the pertinent facts, rights, and liabilities are clear, verification should be made within 15 days of the file of the application. Second, in articles 25 and 29, the revised *Regulations* stipulated a ceiling to the amount of time an evaluation of an employee's suitability for continued service can take. Third, according to article 55 of the revised *Regulations*, the requirement about administrative review is abolished and that in all workplace injury-related disputes, whether they concern the verification request, the verification result, compensation, or premium payments by the employer, the employer and the employee can either apply for administrative review according to the law or file an administrative lawsuit directly with the court (Article 55).

In theory, there is still room for improvements to the system in addition to the above-mentioned revisions. In order to streamline the procedures, the labor administrative agency's responsibilities for establishing the existence of a labor relationship and the employer's duty to cooperate should be emphasized. Establishing the existence of a labor relationship should not have to go through labor arbitration or the courts. As a matter of fact, the labor administrative agency, as the authority charged with verifying work-related injuries, is fully capable of doing so. This would save a lot of time for the parties by obviating the need for them to go through arbitration or the court.

Moreover, according to Article 19 of the *Regulations*, "when the labor administrative agency handles a work-related injury verification application it can conduct investigation in order to verify pertinent facts about the injury-causing accident." In the future, the law should further clarify responsibilities of the labor administrative agency, including the responsibility to establish the existence of a labor relationship. The labor administrative agency should initiate an investigation to ascertain the time, place, causes, and degrees of injury. This is because in many cases of work-related injuries, on one hand, the employer has a strong disincentive to apply for compensation on behalf of their workers because some employers did not enroll them in a workplace injury insurance program to begin with, and on the other the concerned employee are unable to provide convincing evidence proving that the injury is work-related. As such, the labor administrative agency should proactively initiate the investigation in order to reduce the burden on the employee. Also, in order to ensure timely intervention by the labor administrative agency, the duty to report workplace accidents by the employer should be mandatory.

8.4 Work-Related Injuries Compensation for the Uninsured

How work-related injury compensation should be handled when the employer did not enroll their employees in a work-related injury insurance program is an important issue both in theory and in practice. In fact, some employers do not enroll their workers in a workplace injury insurance program. The law before 2010 provided that, under such circumstance, the injured employee could only demand the employer to compensate them directly, that is, out of its own funds. But in practice, many employers refuse or were unable to do so, preventing many injured employees from being compensated and receiving necessary medical treatments in a timely manner. In Theory, work-related injury insurance is a form of mandatory social insurance and administrative agencies must require all employers to enroll their employees in it. When the employer does not comply they are at fault, and the labor administrative agency has also failed in its supervisory duties. Yet the adverse consequences are borne by the employee, which is extremely unfair. In some countries, such as Japan, even if the employee is uninsured, they can still receive work-related injury benefits from the insurance fund in case of a work-related injury. The government has the right to require employers to pay the insurance premium and the compensation either in whole or in part.[9]

In order to redress those situations in which employee are unable to receive compensation because the employer had not enrolled them in an insurance program, the 2010 *Social Insurance Law* stipulated that if an employer has not enrolled their employees in such insurance programs as required by law, they must pay the work-related injury the compensation in cases of injuries sustained by their employees in work-related accidents. If the employer is unable to pay, the workplace injury insurance fund will do so on its behalf and the employer must pay it back later. And if the employer does not pay back the money to insurance fund, a social insurance agency shall make the employer pay through legal procedures.[10] This provision represents

[9] Takashi Araki, *Labor and Employment Law in Japan*, the Japan Institute of Labor, 2002, p. 125.

[10] *Social Insurance Law*, Article 41.

significant progress relative to previous rules and it will help ensure that the injured employee can receive timely compensation when the employer does not pay. Since workers' compensation concerns the life and health of the employee, when the employer fails to enroll their employees in the right insurance programs, it also reflects the failure of regulatory oversight on the part of the labor administrative agencies. Therefore, in order to help the employee, disbursement of compensation payment by the insurance fund should be timely and convenient for the employee to receive. And once the compensation has been paid, it is the labor administrative agency's responsibility to recover from the employer the compensation paid, in addition to the insurance premium.

8.5 Payment of Work-Related Injury Compensation

Once a work-related injury has been verified, the employee is entitled to work-related injury compensation. Under the *Social Insurance Law* and the *Regulations* of 2010, some parts of the compensation shall come from the injury insurance fund and the employer shall cover some expenses. This provision has many Chinese characteristics. In most countries, the law requires the compensation to be drawn from the injury insurance fund and not from the employer's own fund. The Chinese model has its own advantages. On one hand, if employers do not have to pay anything at all in cases of work-related injuries, they would lack the incentive to take workplace safety and accident prevention seriously. This is the rationale behind Chinese laws' requiring even those employers who have enrolled their employees in the insurance program, which frees them from the burden of having to pay the large sum of the compensation, to cover some of the related expenses. On the other hand, not requiring employers to pay the compensation in injury cases makes sense too because doing so would conceivably discourage them from enrolling their workers given the considerable cost associated with (i.e., the insurance premium) and defeats the very purpose of the workplace injury insurance program, namely, to help the employer disperse and lower risks. Letting the injury insurance fund and the employer to share work-related injury liabilities, therefore, appears to be an optimal solution.

The scope of work-related compensation in China is quite similar to that in many countries. For instance, in most states in the U.S., compensation includes medical benefits, disability benefits and death benefits.[11] In Japan, according to the *Employee's Accident Compensation Insurance Law*, work-related injury insurance benefits include medical benefits, welfare benefits during treatment period, disability benefits, survivors' benefits, funeral benefits, injury allowance, and nursing allowance.[12] Of course, the standards of calculation and the relation proportion among the

[11] Mark A. Rothstein, Charles B. Craver, Elinor P. Schroeder, Elaine W. Shoben, *Employment Law*, West, 2005, pp. 672–689.

[12] Takashi Araki, *Labor and Employment Law in Japan*, the Japan Institute of Labor, 2002, pp. 128–129.

different kinds of compensation vary among different countries and regions. The different categories of compensation are more or less the same across countries.

China's *Social Insurance Law* made some adjustments to insurance benefits by expanding the share of payment from the injury insurance fund and reducing that of the employer. The *Social Insurance Law* requires the injury insurance fund to pay for subsidies for food expenditure during hospital stays, and expenditure on transportation and room and board incurred during medical treatment received at healthcare providers other than those participating in the insurance program. The responsibility to pay for these expenditures used to fall on the employer. And upon termination or rescission of the contract because of injury, one-time medical assistance shall also be paid from the insurance fund, as is specified in article 38. Under the *Social Insurance Law*, the following workplace injury related costs still need to be paid by the employer: (1) wages and benefits during treatment; (2) monthly disability allowance for level 5 and level 6 disabilities; and (3) one-time employment disability allowance upon termination or rescission of the contract. There are specified in article 39. But since disability allowance for level 5/6 disabilities, and the one-time employment disability allowance for employees suffering from level 5–10 injuries or disabilities can be considerable, the employer's duty to the injured employee is still rather burdensome.

The 2010 revised *Regulations* increased the amount for some injury benefits, such as the one-time allowance for deaths caused by work-related injuries. The amount for the allowance was too low before, accounting for only 48–60 months of local average wages of the previous year. The revision raised the rate to 20 times the national average of the annual income of the previous year in urban areas and towns. This rate is applied uniformly across the countries and reflects the principle of fairness and equity.

In the meantime, in order to avoid unjustifiably large gaps between treatments of work-related deaths and those of work-related injuries, the revision also increased the one-time work-related disability allowance according to the following rate schedule. For those suffering from levels 1–4 disabilities, the margin of increase is to three months' wage, for those suffering from levels 5/6 disabilities, the margin is two months' wage, and for those suffering from levels 7–10 disabilities, the margin of increase is one month's wage. Under the revised Regulations, the one-time disability allowance are: 27, 25, 23, and 21 months' wage for level-1, 2, 3 and 4 disabilities, respectively; 18 and 16 months' wage for level-5 and level-6 disabilities; and 13, 11, 9, and 7 months' wage for level-7 to level-10 disabilities, respectively. These are specified in articles 35–37 of the revised *Regulations*.

8.6 The Relationship Between Injury Compensation and Tort Damages

Unfortunately, there is no clear provision for the relationship between the injury compensation and torts damages in the *Social Insurance Law* or the *Regulations* of 2010. The Supreme People's Court issued a judicial interpretation in 2003 entitled

The Interpretation of Applicable Laws in Handling Personal Injury Compensation Cases ("*Interpretation*"). According to the *Interpretation*, when an employee suffers a personal injury due to a work-related accident, if the employee or the employee's immediate family brings a lawsuit to the court claiming civil liabilities of the employer, then the employee should be informed that the *Work-related Injury Insurance Regulations* (2003) applies in this situation.[13] In other words, the injured employee is entitled to compensations under the *Social Insurance Law* and the *Work-related Injury Insurance Regulations* instead of tort law. For compensation items not covered by the above *Law* and *Regulations*, the employee is not entitled to damages under the tort law or civil law. That is to say that, work-related injury insurance compensation instead of tort damages will be paid to the employee in this situation. This provision makes a great deal of sense, but also has defects. It makes sense because by entitling employee to work-related injury compensation only, it limits employer liability, which is the very purpose of the injury insurance system. Furthermore, under the Law and the Regulations, the employer must pay a certain amount toward the compensation. Therefore, even if the employee is not entitled to tort damages under the law, the employer is not completely free from liability and the employee can still receive some compensation from them. The defect of the system lies in that the employee cannot obtain damages not covered by the above work-related injury insurance law and regulations, such as mental and emotional damages. By contrast, in some countries, such as Japan, the employee can claim compensations not covered by injury insurance program through civil liability litigation based on tort law or contract law.[14] The employee can file a claim charging the employer with violation of their contractual duty to provide safety and health for the worker. Japan is in this respect different from many countries.

Since the purpose of work-related injury insurance is to disperse the employer's risks and to enable the employee to obtain compensations conveniently, in some sense the injury insurance compensation and tort damages can substitute for each other. The amount of compensation from injury insurance should be increased to bring it closer to the amount of tort damages available. In this way, the employee has easy access to compensations without having to go through both the procedures of administrative claims for workers' compensation and tort litigation. This is also conducive to reducing the employer's risks and saving judicial resources.

As for work injuries caused by a third party, the 2003 Supreme Court *Interpretation* stated that the court should support the employee's claim for civil liability when injured at work by a third party, i.e., a party other than the employer.[15] The *Interpretation* only allows the employee to make tort damages claims to the third party but is unclear about whether the employee is entitled to both injury insurance

[13] *Interpretation of Certain Issues Regarding Application of Laws in Adjudicating Personal Injury Damages Cases*, issued by the Supreme People's Court in 2003, Article 12.

[14] Takashi Araki, *Labor and Employment Law in Japan*, the Japan Institute of Labor, 2002, pp. 130–131.

[15] *Interpretation of Certain Issues Regarding Application of Laws in Adjudicating Personal Injury Damages Cases*, issued by the Supreme People's Court in 2003, Article 12.

compensation and third party tort damages, or if the employee can choose only one of the remedies.

The *Social Insurance Law* has provisions regarding work-related injuries caused by third parties. Article 42 states that "when work-related injury is caused by a third party and the third party does not pay for the medical expenses incurred or the third party cannot be identified, medical expenses can be first paid using money from the work-related injury insurance fund, which has the right to recover it later from the third party." Under this provision it is unclear whether the employee is entitled to both third party tort damages and injury insurance compensation. It is clear that the employee cannot get duplicate compensation for medical expenses, since, after the insurance fund pays the medical expenses, the *Fund* can recover it from the third party (i.e., the third party needs to pay back the money to the *Fund*). But this provision only addresses work-related injury-related medical expenses and is silent regarding whether the employee is entitled to duplicate compensation other than medical expenses, such as disability allowance, compensation for lost wages and nursing expenses, and so forth. Therefore, the *Social Insurance Law* falls short of fully clarifying the issue of compensation for workplace injuries caused by a third party. Hopefully, future judicial or administrative interpretations will do better.

In theory, in dealing with work-related injuries caused by third parties, the substantive rules should reflect three basic principles.

First, the injured employee should have the right to sue the third party and to file insurance compensation claims with the insurance agency. When an employee is injured in the course of employment by a third party's tort conduct, the employee can either receive injury insurance compensation or claim tort damages from the third party in accordance with liability relations. The injured employee should not be deprived of this right from the procedural perspective.

Second, the employee should not receive duplicate compensation. It is not appropriate to allow the employee to obtain both injury insurance compensation and damages from third party for the same items. First, it is not fair or reasonable to allow the employee to be compensated twice over for the same injury. Even though life and health are priceless, the magnitude of losses can be calculated and determined, and duplicate compensation is not reasonable. Second, if employees injured by a third party can receive duplicate compensation and employees injured by a non-third party can only get worker's compensation; it is obviously unfair to the latter. Third, while receives duplicate compensation from the same injury is a good thing for the injured, it is a waste of social resources and injury insurance fund, to some extent.[16] A comparative study shows that duplicate compensation is not allowed in Germany, the U.S., or in Japan.

Third, the injury insurance agency has the right of subrogation after paying the injury insurance benefits. In order to prevent the injured employee from receiving duplicate compensation, some countries give the injury insurance agency the right of subrogation. In Germany, the injury insurance agency can subrogate for tort

[16] Zejian Wang, *Civil Law Theory and Case Studies (Vol.3)*, China University of Political Science and Law Press, 1998, p. 304.

remedies, i.e., it can sue the third party for tort damages.[17] In the U.S., although the varies widely from state to state, the right of the injury insurance agency to sue the third party that caused the injury is protected by the common law and statute laws of most states.[18] In Japan, between the third party's civil liabilities and injury insurance compensation, the civil law "legal subrogation" mechanism is applied by analogy, i.e., the injury insurance agency has the right of subrogation to recover payment toward injury insurance benefits from a third party.[19] In China, the insurance agency's right and the specific procedure of recovering benefits payments from a third party should be further clarified.

[17] Acknowledgement to Professor Rudiger Krause of University of Goettingen for his valuable comments on this issue in 2010.

[18] Gray L. Wickert, *Workers' Compensation Subrogation*, Fourth Edition, Juris Publishing, Inc. 2009, p. 6.

[19] Qian Wei, Jingyi Ye, *Study of Certain Legal Issues Regarding Work-related Injury Compensation System – A Comparative Study of Work-related Injury Compensation System in Japan*. in Social Security, Social Construction, and Social Law – Collection of Papers of 2010 Annual Meeting of China Social Law Association (2nd Vol.), p. 612, Shanghai, August 2010.

Chapter 9
Labor Inspection System and Employer's Liability

9.1 Matters of Labor Inspection

A system of labor inspection of workplaces in agricultural, industrial, commercial and some non-commercial service sectors where workers are employed by the labor inspectorate has been adopted by many countries. The International Labor Organization produces and publishes the international labor standards on labor inspection. Article 2(1) in the ILO *Labor Inspection Convention* (1947, No. 81) states that "the system of labor inspection in industrial workplaces shall apply to all workplaces in respect of which legal provisions relating to conditions of work and the protection of workers while engaged in their work are enforceable by labor inspectors."

According to China's *Labor Law and Labor Contract Law*, the power and the responsibility for labor inspection rest with the labor administration. The Chinese system also has a number of distinct features.

First, the entities subject to labor inspection are employers. According to the law, entities subject to labor inspection mainly include enterprises and individually-owned businesses. In addition, job referral agencies, vocational training agencies, and vocational skills assessment and accreditation agencies are also subject to labor inspection.[1] Thus, the main purpose of labor inspection is to correct breach of labor standards by employers and to safeguard employees' legal rights and interests. The labor inspectorate has no right to inspect employees for law violations. Also, the law requires the labor inspectorate to perform their duties through regular visits, reviewing written requests submitted by employers, and handling complaints.[2]

Second, the scope of the subject matters targeted for inspection is broad. Article 85 of the *Labor Law* is the general provision on labor inspection, and states that "labor administrative agencies in the government above the county-level shall carry

[1] *Labor and Social Security Inspection Regulations*, Article 2.

[2] *Labor and Social Security Inspection Regulations*, Article 14.

Z. Xie, *Labor Law in China*, Research Series on the Chinese Dream and China's Development Path, DOI 10.1007/978-3-662-46929-3_9

out inspection of employers for their compliance with labor laws and regulations, and have the right to order stoppage to and corrections of violations." In 2004, the State Council issued the *Labor and Social Security Inspection Regulations*, which not only detailed the labor administration's responsibilities with respect to labor inspection and enforcement mechanisms but also specified the subject matters to be covered by the inspection. According to the *Regulations*, labor inspection covers the following topics: (1) whether workplace rules and bylaws are consistent with labor laws and standards; (2) whether labor contracts have been signed for all employees; (3) the employer's level of compliance with child labor prohibitions; (4) the employer's level of compliance with special labor rules for the protection of female and minor workers; (5) the employer's level of compliance with rules governing work hours, breaks, and holiday and vacation leaves; (6) wages and implementation of minimum wage standards; (7) if and the variety of social insurance programs the employer offers its employees and its premium payment situation; (8) compliance with government rules and regulations by referral agencies, vocational training agencies, and vocational skills assessment and accreditation agencies; and (9) other topics covered by labor inspection such as prescribed by laws and regulations.[3] Thus, labor inspection cover a wide range work-related topics, including workplace rules and bylaws, labor contracts, use of child labor, protection for women and minority workers, work hours, breaks and holiday and vacation leaves, wages, and social insurance offerings, and so forth.

The 2007 *Labor Contract Law* provides further clarifications on the topics covered by labor, especially those pertaining to labor contracts. Under Article 74 of the *Labor Contract Law*, in addition to the list of topics contained in the *Labor and Social Security Inspection Regulations*, others include the termination of labor contracts and labor dispatching.[4] The labor administrative agency can even target the employer's unfair practice in relation to trade unions for inspection. For instance, the agency can order an employer to make corrections if they have obstructed employees who try to participate in or organize trade unions, obstructed other trade unions who try to assist and guide its employees in establishing trade unions, changed the job positions of trade union officials without justification as retaliation for their performing their duties in accordance with the law, or dismissed an employee for their participation in trade union activities or trade union officials for

[3] *Labor and Social Security Inspection Regulations*, Article 11.

[4] Article 74 of *Labor Contract Law* stipulates: "The labor administrative agency of the local government above county level shall conduct supervision inspection according to law on the following aspects of labor contract implementation: (1) rules and regulations of the employer directly concerning vital interests of the employee and implementation of the rules and regulations; (2) entering and termination of labor contracts between the employer and the employee; (3) compliance of labor dispatch regulations of the labor dispatch agency and the employer; (4) compliance of government regulations on work hours, rest, and holidays; (5) wage remuneration paid according to the labor contract and the minimum wage standards compliance; (6) the employer's participation of various social insurance and premium payments; (7) other matters to be inspected provided by relevant laws and regulations."

their performing their duties in accordance with the law.[5] All these are in violation of the *Trade Union Law*.

We can see, therefore, that in labor inspection in China, a wide range of work-related issues and almost all aspects of the employer's duties is targeted. This may be good for the employee, the intended beneficiaries of these inspections, but it can also generate problems, which will be discussed later.

Third, the labor inspectorate has a wealth of enforcement instruments. According to *Labor and Social Security Inspection Regulations*, when violations are found, the labor inspectorate can order the employer to make corrections, impose fines, order the employer to make remunerations owed to the employee, and even to pay compensation in addition to back pay.[6] While it is necessary for the labor inspectorate to order labor rule violators to make amends and to impose fines, as it is their responsibility to do these, the exact legal status of the imposition by the inspectorate of compensation on top of back pay is still subject to discussion. So is the best division of functions among the labor inspectorate, arbitration agencies, and the courts.

9.2 Effects and Effectiveness of Labor Inspection

Labor inspection has played an important role in labor law enforcement and labor protection in China. Compared to labor arbitration and litigation, labor inspection is a stronger deterrent against labor law violations among employers because of the powerful mandate the law vested in the labor inspectorate. And it is logistically simpler, more convenient, and cheaper for the employee. These are its advantages. For the large number of migrant workers, who tend as a group to be more limited in educational attainment and level of financial literacy, it is often difficult for them to exercise their rights and claim their entitlements through arbitration or litigation. Intervention of the labor inspectorate helps them defend their rights and interests and in particular in claiming back pay. For example, in 2013, China's labor inspectorate visited, on its own initiative, 2.02 million employers for labor inspection across the country, reviewed 2.357 million written documents submitted by employers, processed 419,000 cases of labor and social security violations, helped 5.117 million employees who had been working without a contract to end that situation, helped 4.712 million employees claim back pay or other pay in the amount of 26.85 billion yuan, and saw to it that 94,000 employers make up a total of 3.480 billion yuan in delinquent social security insurance premium payment.[7] These figures are enough to show that labor inspection has played a significant role in protecting the basic rights of the workers.

[5] *Labor and Social Security Inspection Regulations*, Article 29.

[6] *Labor and Social Security Inspection Regulations*, Articles 23–32.

[7] Ministry of Human Resources and Social Security, *Statistical Bulletin of the Development of Human Resources and Social Security Undertaking of 2013*.

9.3 Challenges in Labor Inspection

9.3.1 Topics Targeted for Inspection

Labor inspection in China is very extensive in scope and exhaustive in employment- and labor-related areas. This is good for workers, but both in theory and in practice, its appropriateness may be questionable. Article 3 of the ILO *Labor Inspection Convention* (No. 81) states that "the functions of the system of labor inspection shall be: (a) to secure the enforcement of the legal provisions relating to conditions of work and the protection of workers while engaged in their work, such as provisions relating to hours, wages, safety, health and welfare, the employment of children and young persons, and other connected matters, in so far as such provisions are enforceable by labor inspectors."[8] According to the *Convention*, subject matters to be targeted in labor inspection should be limited to matters concerning the basic rights and interests of the worker, such as work hours, wages, workplace safety, health, welfare, and child labor and youth employment, and the scope of inspection should not be overly expansive. The rationale for this provision of the *Convention* is two-fold: first, given the limited size of its staff, and the large number of employers and employees, covering an extensive list of inspection topics would simply be unmanageable for the labor inspectorate; second, most countries have other legal recourses for labor dispute resolution, and the employee and employer can resolve labor disputes through alternatives such as arbitration or litigation, or other procedures to safeguard their legitimate rights and interests.[9]

We conclude, therefore, that the scope of labor inspections in China could be reduced. For instance, the termination of labor contracts should not be a topic for labor inspection. Termination cases are very complex, involving the determination of whether the employer has legitimate reasons for termination, evidence from both parties, and complicated calculations of severance allowance or damages. It would be more appropriate to leave these issues to arbitration organs or courts to decide. Also, there are huge numbers of labor contract termination cases in China and in other countries alike. The administrative agency will be over-burdened if it must handle all or even many of them. For example, in 2012, 92 % of labor dispute cases in Beijing were about wages and contract termination.[10] This supports the position that termination cases are not suitable for handling by labor inspection agencies.

Further, entrusting the labor administration with too many inspection items can increase risks to the agency. In reality, many employees request the agency to order the employer to make up back pay and pay severance allowance. If the agency decides not to support the employee's claim in accordance with Article 21 of the

---

[8] Article 3(1) of *Labor Inspection Convention*, 1947.

[9] Zengyi Xie, *Study of the Administrative Agency Ordering the Employer to Bear Civil Liabilities*, Contemporary Law Review, 2010, No. 3, p. 114.

[10] *Labor and Social Security*, edited by Beijing Labor and Social Security Law Society, 2013, No. 3, pp. 26–27.

Labor and Social Security Inspection Regulations,[11] the employee could bring a lawsuit against the agency for inaction, and the agency frequently loses in such cases.[12] Thus, over-expansion of inspection items will not only overwhelm the agency, but may also subject the agency to greater and sometimes unnecessary risks.

9.3.2 Shortage of Labor Inspectors

By the end of 2013, there were 3,291 labor and social security inspection agencies throughout the country with 25,000 full-time labor inspectors serving in the Human Resources and Social Security department at various levels.[13] There is an acute shortage of labor inspectors, given the much larger number of enterprises and individually-owned businesses and or employees. According to one statistic, by the end of September 2013, there were a total of 14.6931 million enterprises in China, and 43.1157 million individually-owned businesses.[14] Statistics from the Ministry of Human Resources and Social Security show that by the end of 2013, a total of 769.77 million people were employed nationwide, of which 382.40 million worked in cities and towns, and 268.94 million were migrant workers.[15] The number of labor inspection agencies and inspectors obviously pales in comparison.

Due to this acute shortage, much of labor inspection is actually done passively, i.e. by way of processing complaints. Agencies rarely visit workplaces on their own initiative to conduct inspection, which compromises the effectiveness of labor supervision. For instance, in 2010, labor and social security inspection agencies processed 384,000 violation cases, of which 336,000 were complaints and reports, which accounted for 87.5 % of the total. In 2011 and 2012, the percentages of violations handled through processing complaints and reports were 91.3 % and 88.8 %,

---

[11] Article 21 of *Labor and Social Inspection Regulations* stipulates: When the employer causes harm to the employee in violation of labor and security laws and regulations, the employer has an obligation to pay damages according to law. If there is a dispute about the damages, it should be handled according to the government's regulation regarding labor dispute resolution. For matters that should be resolved through labor dispute resolution procedures, or matters already applied for mediation, or arbitration, or a lawsuit has been filed, the labor administrative agency should inform the complainant to pursue the matter according to labor dispute resolution procedures.

[12] Yujuan Zhai, *The Plight and Challenges of Labor Inspection in China – Examples of the Labor Administrative Agency Losing the Case Frequently*, Administration and Law, 2008, No. 5, p. 76.

[13] Ministry of Human Resources and Social Security, *Statistical Bulletin of the Development of Human Resources and Social Security Undertaking of* 2013.

[14] National Administration of Industry and Commerce: *Nationwide Major Market Development Report*, 3rd Quarter, 2013. See website http://www.saic.gov.cn/zwgk/tjzl/zhtj/bgt/201310/P020131015377705296718.pdf.

[15] Ministry of Human Resources and Social Security, *Statistical Bulletin of the Development of Human Resources and Social Security Undertaking of* 2013.

respectively.[16] This means that about 90 % of violations are handled through processing complaint reports. The percentage of violation cases discovered by and then actively pursued by the agencies was low, possibly undermining the effectiveness of labor inspection.

9.3.3 Relationship Between Labor Inspection and Other Forms of Remedy

Labor inspection can correct certain violations committed by employers and protect employees' rights. Alternatively, under Chinese law, employees can also seek remedy through labor arbitration and litigation. Therefore, it is necessary to clarify the extent of a labor agency's involvement and the relationship among labor inspection, arbitration, and litigation. Take an employment discrimination case for example. An individual surnamed Tao applied for a job in a company in 2010. The company ordered Tao to undergo a physical examination and the he was tested positive for Hepatitis B. The company refused to hire Tao on that ground. Tao then filed a complaint with a labor inspection agency accusing the company of employment discrimination and requested the agency to order the company either to hire and sign a labor contract with him, or to pay him for damage due to lost wages. The labor inspection agency investigated the case immediately after receiving the complaint and determined that the job position to which Tao applied does not fall in the category of jobs in which Hepatitis B pathogen carriers are legally prohibited from working. It was then decided that the employer had violated the *Employment Promotion Law* and *Employment Service and Management Regulations* in ordering this test for prospective employees. The agency ordered the employer to rescind the rejection letter to Tao and pay a fine in the amount of 500 yuan.[17]

But there were questions about how to handle with Mr. Tao's other requests. First, can the labor inspection agency order the employer to sign a labor contract with Tao? Or is this something for which Tao must turn to arbitration agencies or the courts instead? Second, if Tao refused to work for the employer, could the inspection agency order the employer to pay damages to Tao, or would Tao have to turn to arbitration agencies or the courts to claim that?[18] This case raised an important issue about what the labor inspection agency can, and cannot do in labor inspection and its relationship with labor arbitration organs or courts in handling labor cases. In practice, labor administrative agencies would normally issues orders to the employer directly regarding wage, severance allowance, and the minimum wage. They do not

---

[16] Ministry of Human Resources and Social Security, *Statistical Bulletin of the Development of Human Resources and Social Security Undertaking of* 2010, 2011, 2012.

[17] Hui Sun, *How Does Labor Inspection Handle Employment Discrimination Casesn*, China Labor, 2010, No. 11, pp. 55–56.

[18] Hui Sun, *How Does Labor Inspection Handle Employment Discrimination Casesn*, China Labor, 2010, No. 11, pp. 55–56.

decide on matters related to other duties and obligations of the employer toward the employee. Thus, it needs to be clarified in which areas the labor administration can order violators to make amendments and what powers the agency should have in labor inspection.

9.4 The Power of the Labor Inspectorate and Employers' Liabilities

9.4.1 Ordering Employers to Meet Their Obligations

Since the subject matters covered by labor inspection include those related to the basic rights of the employee such as that to wage/remuneration, the law has imposed rather harsh liabilities on employers for violations. Article 85 of the *Labor Contract Law* provides that the labor inspectorate can order a violator to assume certain liabilities in addition to meeting its legal obligations. According to Article 85:

> [I]in one of the following situations the labor administrative agency can order the employer to pay remuneration, overtime, or severance allowance within certain time frame; if the rate of remuneration is lower than the local minimum wage, the shortfall shall be paid; if payment is not made after the deadline, an additional compensation of over 50% and below 100% of the due amount could be ordered. The situations are: (1) the employer fails to timely pay the full amount of labor remuneration in accordance with the labor contract or government regulations; (2) the remuneration is lower than the local minimum wage standard; (3) overtime is not paid after the employee is assigned to overtime work; (4) severance allowance is not paid according provisions of this law when labor contract is rescind or terminated.

Here language is complex and has two layers of meaning. On one, it says that if the inspectorate decides that an employer has violated its legal or contractual duty of payment, the agency can order the employer to make up the payments to the employee. Under these circumstances, the employer is fulfilling its statutory compensatory obligation; On the other, this article says that if the employer fails to meet their obligations within the deadline set by the agency, the latter can impose a penalty in the amount of 50–100 % of what is owed the employee to be paid in addition to it, which is a liability of punitive damages against the employer.[19] This raises the important question of whether the law has given the labor agency too much power, whether the labor agency should have the power to order the employer to take a punitive liability, or if such liability should be decided only by arbitration organs or the courts.

---

[19] It is very important to make certain distinctions regarding this provision. The administrative agency can only order punitive damages after the employer's failure of fulfilling the agency's previous order of correction. It means that the administrative agency cannot order the employer to bear punitive damages directly. This is important in both practice and theory.

9.4.2 Improving the Employer's Liability in Labor Inspection

Following general legal theory, when an employer fails to make timely and full wage or minimum wage payment to an employee, the labor administrative agency can order the employer to do so, which is the proper function of the agency. But if the employer fails to make the payment by the deadline and fails to file for administrative review or administrative litigation, whether the labor inspection agency can require the employer to pay extra punitive damages is doubtful. As an administrative agency, usually the labor inspectorate can only require that the employer to fulfill its duties to the employee. When the employer fails to do so, the agency can impose a fine or other forms of penalty. But punitive damages are usually imposed by the courts or other judicial organs. Ordering the party to pay punitive damages seems not in line with the nature of an administrative agency.

Therefore, Article 85 of the current should be revised. In theory, if the employer fails to pay the employee in full and in a timely manner, or if the wages paid are below the local minimum wage, or if the employee fails to pay for overtime, or if severance allowance is not paid when a labor contract is rescinded or terminated, the labor inspection agency can decide to require the employer to fulfill its obligations. If the employer fails to do so, the labor inspection agency can impose fines on the employer. In addition, the employee can also demand that the employer fulfill its obligations based on the labor contract or the law through arbitration or litigation procedure.

Chapter 10
Labor Dispute Resolution

The *Labor Dispute Mediation and Arbitration Law* was passed in China in 2007 and became effective May 1, 2008. The law made some progress on the mechanism for labor dispute resolution, but there are still controversies, and further improvements are needed.

10.1 Necessity of Establishing a Special Labor Dispute Resolution Mechanism

In many countries, general civil dispute procedure is not applicable to labor dispute resolution and labor disputes are not handled directly by regular courts. The necessity of a special labor dispute resolution mechanism is due to the special features of labor relationships and labor disputes, especially the imbalance in status between the employer and the employee.

First, establishing a labor dispute resolution mechanism that is relatively independent of the general civil dispute resolution procedure is conducive to reducing antagonism and maintaining an amiable relationship between the employer and employee. Labor relationships are different from other types of civil relationships. The employee often must work at the place provided by the employer and accept the direction and supervision of the latter. They have a close relationship and it is crucial to keep it amiable. If a lawsuit is brought to court whenever there is a dispute, the relationship is likely to be damaged and the problem escalated. Especially in disputes involving wages, social insurance, employment discrimination, and dismissal, the labor relationship may continue during the dispute. If the relationship is poor or becomes broken, it would be difficult to maintain the work relationship, which can be detrimental to both parties. Especially in cases of collective disputes, if they are not resolved through negotiation and settlement but by court ruling, and one party is dissatisfied with it, it may seriously affect the labor relationship.

Z. Xie, *Labor Law in China*, Research Series on the Chinese Dream and China's Development Path, DOI 10.1007/978-3-662-46929-3_10

Therefore, it is necessary to set up a special mechanism to enable the parties to resolve disputes in amicably way.

Second, a special dispute resolution mechanism can help reduce the imbalance in power and status between the employer and employee. When a labor dispute occurs, the employee is often unable to maintain their normal work schedule and may suffer loss of wages, social security, and other benefits. In comparison, loss to the employer tends to be minor. The employee is at an obvious disadvantage. And the disadvantage would continue during the litigation process due to the employee's lack of experience in meeting the burden of proof and of financial resources. Experienced attorneys are expensive, and often times only the employer but not the employee can afford them. And because the litigation does not represent a large burden on the employer, they can afford to pursue complicated appeals proceedings. And some employers even intentionally adopt a marathon litigation strategy in order to wear out the employee, who invariably hopes to see a quick resolution and to avoid more losses. Handling disputes through regular litigation proceedings puts employee at a distinct disadvantage. Therefore, free mediation services, simple arbitration procedure or other simple procedure can help expedite dispute resolution and to mitigate the employee's losses and disadvantages in litigation.

Third, the special dispute resolution mechanism can help reduce the caseloads of courts. Given the ubiquity of labor relationships, and the large numbers of employees and labor disputes, if all labor disputes end up in the court, it is not only unfavorable to the employee, but will also overwhelm the court system. For example, in 2013, various mediation and labor arbitration agencies in China handled 1,497,000 cases of labor disputes.[1] If all these cases had gone to court instead, the courts would have become inundated.

Fourth, establishing a special dispute resolution mechanism can help enhance professionalism in case-handling by engaging people with special knowledge and experience in labor relations to participate in the process. Since labor disputes may touch upon any part of the labor relationship, participation by representatives of the employer and the employee can help the parties to have a better understanding of each other's positions and demands. This helps facilitate timely settlements. If, on the contrary, the cases are handled by regular courts, the court would usually apply the principle of private autonomy in civil law or contract law without consideration for special labor law theories and the special needs to protect the employee, and the ruling could be unfavorable to the employee. In common law countries, common law principles are usually different from labor statutes, and applying common law theories to adjudication of labor disputes may not fulfill the legislative intent of the statute. Therefore, creating special employment tribunals or other mechanism will help to enforce the labor statutes rather than the common law or contract laws, providing stronger protection for the employee.

In short, a labor dispute resolution mechanism reflects the purposes of public policies of a country, such as maintaining a cooperative relationship between the employer and the employee in order to increase economic efficiency, reducing liti-

[1] Ministry of Human Resources and Social Security, *Statistical Bulletin of the Development of Human Resources and Social Security Undertaking of 2013*.

gation costs and other economic losses, helping the employee stabilize their work relationship, and reducing the imbalance of power between the employer and the employee. Based on these policy considerations, the best approach should be to settle labor disputes through low-cost and faster non-litigation alternative dispute resolution (ADR) mechanisms as much as possible. This is the basic rationale for establishing a special labor dispute resolution mechanism and the principle behind China's choice in the model of labor dispute resolution.

10.2 Labor Dispute Resolution in Some Countries

10.2.1 The U.K.

As a country that completed industrialization early, the U.K. has rich experience in resolving labor disputes through a comprehensive and effective system which includes internal consultation with the employer, external mediation, arbitration, special employment tribunal, employment appeal tribunal, and common law court proceedings.

10.2.1.1 Employment Tribunal

In the U.K., judicial organs for labor disputes resolution include the employment tribunal and common law courts. The employment tribunal primarily handles disputes involving rights created by statues, while the courts handle disputes involving contracts and torts. Most complaints filed by the employee against employers for violation of the employee's statutory rights or violation of statutory standards fall within the jurisdiction of the employment tribunal. The tribunal has a "tripartite" structure, consisting of three tribunal adjudicators. The presiding adjudicator is a barrister or solicitor appointed by the Lord Chancellor, and the other two adjudicators are lay members drawn through appointment from special recommended groups of the employer and employee.[2] The purpose of having two members other than the lawyer participate is to equip the tribunal with people who have practical knowledge of and experience with labor relationship. As with other tribunals, the employment tribunal also hopes to have the disputes resolved through an informal and less cumbersome procedure and by reaching a settlement agreement between the parties.

If the parties are dissatisfied with the "matter of law" decided by the employment tribunal, they can file an appeal with the Employment Appeal Tribunal. The appeal tribunal is also tripartite, consisting of lay persons representing the employer and the employee and one judge appointed by the high or appellate court.[3]

---

[2] *Employment Tribunals Act* 1996, Sec. 4.

[3] Deborah Lockton, *Employment Law* (Fourth Edition), Palgrave Macmillan, 2003, p. 12.

In practice, the court still plays an important role in resolving labor disputes. Apart from continuing to have the power of issuing orders of injunction in collective labor actions, the court also serves as a court of final appeal if the parties are dissatisfied with the ruling by the Employment Appeal Tribunal. The parties can file appeals with the Court of Appeal and from there with the House of Lords based on an "error of law" in the ruling by the Employment Appeal Tribunal. The power of accepting appeals gives the court an opportunity to provide authoritative interpretations of the statutes that give rights to workers as well as to supervise the employment tribunal.[4]

10.2.1.2 Labor Mediation

The British government set up an independent labor dispute mediation mechanism in 1975, the Advisory, Conciliation and Arbitration Service, or ACAS.[5] Its mission statement declared: "ACAS provides free and impartial information and advice to employers and employees on all aspects of workplace relations and employment law. We support good relationships between employers and employees which underpin business. But when things go wrong we can also help by providing conciliation to help resolve workplace problems. We also provide good value, high quality training and tailored advice to employers." [6] Although ACAS must submit an annual report to the Secretary of State,[7] the law clearly states that ACAS shall perform its function independently of government instructions.[8] Therefore, ACAS has the characteristics of a quasi-judicial body. In practice, it not only conducts mediation but can also give its opinions to disputing parties on how to improve labor relations. According to the law, the ACAS has the legal duty to promote amiable labor relations.[9]

(1) Mediation of Individual Disputes

According to statutory provisions, mediation procedures apply to most cases submitted to the Employment Tribunal. Once a dispute is filed with the Tribunal, the Tribunal will give a copy of the complaint to ACAS.[10] In fact, ACAS has a mandatory mediation function in many individual labor disputes, such as wrongful termination, discrimination, equal remuneration, wage protection, breach of contract, minimum wage, and work hours. Under the provisions of the 1996 Employment Tribunals

---

[4] Huge Collins, K.D. Ewing and Aileen McColgan, *Labor law: Text and Materials*, Hart Publishing, Oxford and Portland, Oregon, 2005, pp. 31–32.

[5] See, http://www.acas.org.uk.

[6] Http://www.acas.org.uk/index.aspx?articleid=1342.

[7] *Trade Union and Labor Relations (Consolidation) Act* 1992, Sec 253(1).

[8] *Trade Union and Labor Relations (Consolidation) Act* 1992, Sec. 247 (3).

[9] *Trade Union and Labor Relations (Consolidation) Act* 1992, Sec. 209.

[10] *The Employment Tribunals (Constitution and Rules of Procedure) Regulations* 2004 (SI 2004/1861) Schedule 1, para 21.

Act, when the applicant brings a complaint to the Tribunal, or either the applicant or the respondent requires a mediation, or none of the parties makes such a request but the mediator believes there is a good chance of reaching a settlement, then ACAS should try its best to realize that and to avoid a court decision.[11] And the parties cannot refuse to cooperate in the mediation process. All discussions in mediation are confidential, and more importantly, the service is free. In practice, mediators of ACAS participate in almost all individual labor disputes filed with the Tribunal. For instance, in 2011–2012, ACAS successfully resolved 79 % of such disputes so the cases didn't have to be decided by the Tribunal.[12]

(2) Mediation of Collective Disputes

ACAS also provides mediation service to "trade union disputes" that have occurred or are likely to occur. "Trade union disputes" include those between the employer and employees, and those among employees.[13] One party, or both parties, can request mediation; ACAS can also take the initiative to mediate.[14] No matter how the process is initiated, mediation of collective disputes is entirely voluntary and any party can withdraw at any stage during the process. Before offering the mediation service, ACAS must fully respect the negotiation or dispute resolution procedure agreements reached by the parties. In 2011–2012, ACAS handled 943 collective labor disputes, among which 754 cases were resolved successfully and 113 cases were withdrawn.[15] This shows the high success rate of ACAS's mediation.

The most significant feature of the British system is that a complex and sound labor dispute resolution mechanism exists outside the court system, which helps to resolve labor disputes in a timely and just manner through alternative dispute resolution methods such as mediation.

10.2.2 Germany

In Germany, labor courts are the main bodies for individual and collective labor dispute resolution. There are labor courts in the first instance, which serve as trial courts and labor courts in the second instance, which serve as appellate courts for handling appeals based on matters of facts and law. The federal courts sit above these two courts and only handle appeals based on matters of law. First instance labor courts consist of a professional judge and two lay judges who are

[11] *Employment Tribunals Act* 1996 Sec 18(2).

[12] ACAS Annual Report & Accounts 2011/12, p. 13. http://acas.ecgroup.net/Publications/Accounts.aspx.

[13] *Trade Union and Labor Relations (Consolidation) Act* 1992, Sec. 218.

[14] *Trade Union and Labor Relations (Consolidation) Act* 1992, Sec. 210.

[15] ACAS Annual Report & Accounts 2011/12, p. 48. http://acas.ecgroup.net/Publications/Accounts.aspx.

representatives of the employer and the employee, respectively. Second-instance appellate labor courts also consist of a professional judge and two lay judges who are representatives of the employer and the employee, respectively.[16] The composition of the labor courts demonstrates a clear "tripartite" structure and a strong administrative character.

Labor courts play a comprehensive role in resolving labor disputes, especially individual disputes. They have exclusive jurisdiction over disputes between the employer and the employee, including those over the validity of a labor contract relationship, legal obligations upon termination of contracts, and labor-related torts. The 1957 revised *Labor Courts Law* modified the general rules that applied in civil courts and provided a convenient, expedited, and low-cost procedure for labor courts. Labor courts will first deploy mediation procedures and cases will only enter trial proceedings when the parties fail to reach a settlement. Labor courts also have comprehensive and exclusive jurisdiction over collective labor disputes. But the procedure applied in collective labor disputes is different from that for individual disputes.[17]

10.2.3 Japan

In Japan, there are no special courts for handling labor disputes. But there are many labor dispute resolution agencies outside the court system. The Ministry of Health, Labor, and Welfare was established in 2001. Several bureaus within the Ministry are in charge of labor law implementation. The Ministry also established 47 Prefectural Labor Bureaus for labor law enforcement. The Labor Standards Bureau within the Ministry is responsible for implementing labor standards established by the labor laws. Apart from labor administrative agencies at the central government level, local governments also have labor offices that provide consultation, mediation for individual and collective labor disputes and other administrative support.[18] In 2004, the *Labor Trial Law* was passed in Japan, which introduced the system of labor tribunals within the court. The labor tribunals are composed of a professional judge and two lay persons with labor law knowledge recommended by the employee and the employer. The labor tribunals are in charge of individual labor disputes and using a simpler procedure to handle the cases.

In addition to these administrative agencies, Japan also has a Central Labor Relations Commission and Local Labor Relations Commissions that handle only

---

[16] Blanpain, Bisom Rapp, Corbett, Josephs, and Zimmer, *The Global Workplace: International and Comparative Employment Law: Cases and Materials*, Cambridge University Press, 2007, p. 429.

[17] Blanpain, Bisom-Rapp, Corbett, Josephs, and Zimmer, *The Global Workplace: International and Comparative Employment Law: Cases and Materials*, Cambridge University Press, 2007, pp. 429–430.

[18] Takashi Araki, *Labor and Employment Law in Japan*, The Japan Institute of Labor, 2002, pp. 12–13.

collective labor disputes. These commissions are independent and composed of an equal number of employers, employees, and representatives of public interests. In order to strengthen mediation for individual labor disputes Japan adopted the *Individual Labor Disputes Resolution Law*, which enabled Prefectural Labor Bureaus to play a greater role in individual labor dispute mediation. Therefore, despite there being no special labor courts in Japan, administrative agencies play an important role in giving advice and guidance and especially in providing mediation.

We can see that the labor dispute resolution mechanisms in the U.K., Germany, and Japan have some common features. First, there is a special labor dispute resolution mechanism outside the regular court system; second, great emphasis is given to mediation, making it an important means for labor dispute resolution; third, the structure of part dispute resolution agencies is tripartite, made up of representatives of the employer, the employee, and the government.

10.3 Labor Dispute Resolution in China

10.3.1 Labor Arbitration

10.3.1.1 Characteristics of Labor Arbitration

According to China's *Labor Law,* when a labor dispute occurs, the parties can either apply for mediation or directly for arbitration, and if dissatisfied with the arbitration decision, a lawsuit can be filed.[19] Therefore, arbitration is a prerequisite for litigation and the parties cannot sue in court directly. This shows the importance of labor arbitration, which is a significant feature of China's labor dispute resolution mechanism.

The *Labor Dispute Mediation and Arbitration Law* improved the resolution mechanism in many ways. Compared to court proceedings, labor arbitration has several advantages. First, the arbitration agency is a "tripartite" body. The Labor Dispute Arbitration Commission consists of representatives of the labor administrative agency, the trade union, and the enterprise, and the Commission engages the representatives as arbitrators.[20] The Commission is independent to a certain degree, but is also under the guidance of the labor administrative agency. Second, the procedure for the resolution mechanism is simpler than litigation procedures. The statute of limitations for arbitration requests is one year, which is relatively short.[21] In addition, a labor dispute for arbitration should usually be completed within 45 days of the date of filing of arbitration application.[22] For certain types of small

---

[19] *Labor Law,* Article 79.

[20] *The Labor Dispute Mediation and Arbitration Law,* Article 18, 19.

[21] *The Labor Dispute Mediation and Arbitration Law,* Article 27.

[22] *The Labor Dispute Mediation and Arbitration Law,* Article 43.

claims, the arbitration decision will be final and binding, and the employer cannot appeal to the court.[23] Third, the burden of proof is special. The employee is responsible for providing evidence to support his or her own claim, but if relevant evidence is under the control of the employer, then the employer must provide the evidence; failure to do so will lead to a result unfavorable to the employer.[24] Fourth, the arbitration is free.[25] The expenses of arbitration commissions are borne by the government, and employees do not need to pay.

10.3.1.2 Cases Handled by Labor Arbitration

Before the *Labor Contract Law* was introduced, for various reasons, the number of labor disputes had been rising rapidly. According to the statistics from the Ministry of Labor and Social Security, in the 12 years from 1995 through 2006, the numbers of labor disputes and collective labor disputes cases increased by 13.5 and 5.4 times, respectively.[26]

There has been a sharp increase in the number of labor dispute cases since 2008. Between then and now, several labor laws have become effective, such as the *Labor Contract Law* and its Implementation Regulations, *Labor Dispute Mediation and Arbitration Law, Employment Promotion Law,* and *Regulations of Workers Annual Paid Leave.* In 2010, arbitration agencies at various levels handled 601,000 labor disputes, of which 9,000 cases were collective labor disputes. And the number of labor disputes handled by various arbitration agencies and collective labor disputes for 2011 and 2012 stood at 589,000 and 7,000, and then 641,000 and 7,000, respectively.[27] Arbitration helped greatly to reduce the caseload of the courts. Take Beijing as an example. In 2012, the courts in Beijing received 20,540 new labor dispute cases for first instance,[28] and by contrast arbitration agencies in Beijing handled 66,463 labor disputes in the same year.[29] This means that the number of labor cases handled by the court was 31 % of the number handled by arbitration agencies. In yet other words, two-thirds or nearly 70 % of labor disputes were resolved through arbitration. Evidently arbitration has been effective in preventing labor dispute cases from overwhelming the courts.

---

[23] *The Labor Dispute Mediation and Arbitration Law,* Article 47.

[24] *The Labor Dispute Mediation and Arbitration Law,* Article 6.

[25] *The Labor Dispute Mediation and Arbitration Law,* Article 53.

[26] The Interpretation on *Labor Contract Law* by The Director of the Law Committee of the National People's Congress, Xinua website: http://www.xinhuanet.com/zhibo/20070723/wz.htm.

[27] Ministry of Human Resources and Social Security, *Statistical Bulletin of Human Resources and Social Security Development Situation of 2010, 2011, 2012.*

[28] Beijing Labor and Social Security Law Society (ed.), *Labor and Social Security,* 2013, No. 3, p. 18.

[29] Beijing Labor and Social Security Law Society (ed.), *Labor and Social Security,* 2013, No. 3, p. 26.

10.3.1.3 Challenges Facing Labor Arbitration

Still, there are problems in labor arbitration that arbitration agencies need to pay attention to. First, the *Labor Dispute Mediation and Arbitration Law* stipulated that the structuring of arbitration agencies should follow the "tripartite" principle, but this is not always the case in practice. Representatives from trade unions and enterprises rarely participate in arbitration, and the arbitrators are mostly members of the staff from labor administrative agencies. Second, arbitration agencies are not fully independent. Labor administrative agencies are responsible for the daily operations of labor dispute arbitration commissions. Thus, the commissions have a strong administrative flavor and lack full independence. Recently, an increasing number of labor arbitration agencies have become labor arbitration courts, giving them greater independence from the labor agencies. Third, arbitration agencies exhibit weak professionalism. Some arbitrators in basic-level arbitration agencies are not legal professionals. Professional standards for full-time arbitrators are lower than those for lawyers, judges, and prosecutors. There are no national professional qualification exams for arbitrators.[30]

10.3.1.4 Controversies Surrounding "Finality of Arbitration Decisions" for Certain Cases

According to, the *Labor Dispute Mediation and Arbitration Law*, in certain cases, arbitration decisions are final, i.e., they cannot be appealed. Under the *Law*, such cases include disputes over labor remuneration, workplace injury-related medical expenses, severance allowance or damages in termination of contracts, cases in which the amounts in dispute do not exceed 12 times the local monthly minimum wage, and disputes over implementation of national labor standards regarding work hours, breaks and holiday and vacation leaves, and social insurance. In these cases, if the employee is dissatisfied with the arbitration decision, they can sue in the court. However, if the employer is dissatisfied with the arbitration decision, they cannot. The employer must first petition the court on legitimate grounds to cancel the arbitration award and it is only when the petition is approved and the award cancelled can the employer file a lawsuit with the court. This imposes considerable constraints on the employer's ability to appeal the case.[31] Therefore, in these types of labor disputes, if the employee does not sue in court within the statute of limitation and the employer's petition for cancellation of the arbitration award is denied, then the arbitration decision becomes final. The background to this rule is that, in practice, many employers abuse the availability of both the arbitration and litigation options to take unfair advantage of the employees. Therefore, the finality of the arbitration decision in some cases can benefit employees by preventing some employers from

[30] Bei Wang, *The Defects and Improvements of China's Labor Dispute Arbitration Mechanism,* Academic Journal of Hebei University (Philosophy and Social Science), 2013, No. 3, p. 80.

[31] *The Labor Dispute Mediation and Arbitration Law,* Article 47, 48, 49.

engaging in abusive practices and help speed on processing. The system is not without problems. I discuss some of them below.

First, this mechanism grants the employee the right to sue but imposes considerable constraints on the employer's ability to do the same. This creates an *ipso facto* inequality and indefensible from a theoretical point of view. Although the employer may abuse the right to sue and the employer is usually in a more powerful position in a labor relationship, employees are not beyond abusing their right to sue. Therefore, restricting the employer's right to sue but not that of the employee is unjustified.

Second, the finality of arbitration decisions is not in line with common practice. In many countries and regions, when the parties are dissatisfied with the decision of a special labor dispute resolution agency, any one of them is allowed to sue in court. Any suit in court, however, is basically limited to "matters of law," and only parties of high impact lawsuits can appeal to the higher court if dissatisfied with the decision of the trial court. This helps to strike a balance between the need to ensure parity in the rights to sue and that to expedite the handling of cases. The parties can at least appeal "matter of law" issues to the court. In China, however, the finality of arbitration decisions for smaller claims is overly restrictive of the employer's right to appeal the case from arbitration agencies with courts.

Third, the types of cases and standards to which restrictions on the right to sue are applicable are over-simplified. Cases with smaller claims are not necessarily simple, just like cases with big claims are not necessarily complex. Cases with smaller claims may involve complex legal issues. Therefore, using the claim amount as the standard for restriction is ill-advised. For instance, the issue of severance allowance or damages in the termination of labor contracts is very complex, and over-restriction on the employer's right to sue for these types of cases is not reasonable.

Lastly, China's current crop of a labor arbitrators lack both capability and experience. As such excessive restriction of the employer's right to sue would to some extent deprive the court the ability to exercise oversight concerning arbitration awards in many cases.

A data indicates that the practice of allowing arbitration decisions to be final has not greatly reduced labor lawsuits. The reasons are twofold. First, most cases fall below the threshold and are not covered by the rule. When the employee sued in court, a single claim would usually far exceed the legal limit of 12 times of local monthly minimum wage, and thus the finality rule does not apply for a large number of cases. Second, the cost of labor litigation is extremely low, which encourages the employee to sue. In China, the litigation fee to file a labor dispute is usually only 10 yuan, and the fee can be reduced, waived, or payment-deferred for low-income employees. Affordability alone makes suing in court attractive for many employees.[32] This means that the rule of finality for arbitration decisions in some cases is not only unjustified, but also little used in practice.

[32] Ling Tan, *Current Plight and Future Transition of One Arbitration as the Final Ruling for Labor Dispute Cases,* People's Justice, 2012, No.1, p. 69.

Reforms in the future should ensure parity in the right to sue for both the employee and the employer. Both parties should be able to bring an action regarding a matter of law currently in arbitration to the court. Then, the parties should be allowed to appeal to the higher court only if the case involves serious and major legal issues.

10.3.2 Labor Litigation

According to the law, parties can sue in court if dissatisfied with the arbitration award. China does not have special labor courts and regular courts for handling labor cases.

In general, labor law cases are treated as one type of civil cases and the general rules of civil procedure apply. Also, under the *Code of Civil Procedures*, the ruling of the second trial is final for labor cases. Although the court handles appeals from arbitrations, it can conduct a comprehensive review of the facts and matters of law. And if the parties are dissatisfied with a decision in the first instance, an appeal can be filed with a court of the second instance. According to statistics, in 2010, labor disputes that ended in litigation totaled 327,407 nationwide.[33] While this is a large number, the number of cases that ended in courts of the first and second instances was only about half of the number of cases handled by arbitration agencies.[34] There are two main challenges facing labor litigation procedures: first, general labor litigation is treated as one type of civil litigation, and judges tend to apply civil law or private law principles in labor cases, which might not be favorable to the employee; secondly, labor litigation procedures can be complex, with two instances of trial, where both legal and factual issues are reviewed. Thus, the parties may have to go through arbitration and two trials procedures, which can delay resolution in some cases.

10.3.3 Labor Mediation

Mediation has played an important role in labor dispute resolution. All local governments have established mediation or special labor mediation organizations. According to the *Labor Dispute Mediation and Arbitration Law,* when a labor dispute occurs, the parties can turn to the following organizations for mediation: (1) labor dispute mediation committee within the concerned enterprise; (2) grassroots people's mediation organization; and (3) agencies at the rural township and urban

---

[33] Bei Wang, *Labor Dispute Mediation: Case Analysis and Suggestions for Reform,* Social Science Study, 2012, No.6, p. 85.

[34] Ministry of Human Resources and Social Security, *Statistical Bulletin of the Development of Human Resources and Social Security Undertaking of 2010.*

sub-district level that have mediation functions.[35] According to statistics from the Ministry of Human Resources and Social Security, from 2010 to 2012, mediation organizations in China (including mediation in outside arbitration agencies) handled 685,000, 726,000, and 762,000 cases, respectively,[36] which exceeded the number handled by arbitration agencies. Actually, mediation is not only deployed by mediation organizations in handling labor disputes, but also by arbitration agencies and courts in resolving labor disputes. Currently, the main issue facing mediation organizations is the low level of professionalism and the lack of financial support. Grassroots people's mediation organizations lack legal authority due to inadequacy in professional skills, especially for handling complicated labor disputes. Some regional or trade-wide labor dispute mediation organizations lack sufficient funding.[37]

10.3.4 Collective Labor Dispute Resolution

Most labor arbitration cases in China are individual disputes. The percentage of collective disputes out of the total is very low. Although in labor arbitration there are some collective disputes, those cases in essence are a combination of a large number of individual disputes, and not genuine "collective disputes" such as those given rise to the organization of a trade union or the signing and execution of collective agreements. In China, there are not many real collective labor disputes and their handling procedures are relatively simple. Under the *Labor Law,* disputes involving execution of collective agreements can be resolved through arbitration and/or litigation. The provision for how to resolve disputes involving the signing of collective agreements is very simple. It only states that the dispute should be resolved by the labor administrative agency through coordination with all relevant parties. It is not clear who the relevant parties are, how to coordinate, or what procedures should be followed. Therefore, future improvement in China's labor dispute resolution mechanisms should focus on collective dispute resolution.

10.4 Controversies Regarding Labor Dispute Resolution Model and Its Improvements

The "Singular arbitration decision, dual trials" model of labor dispute resolution, i.e., the model in which compulsory arbitration is followed by two trials, of the first and the second instances, has been highly controversial. It was the subject of intense

[35] *The Labor Dispute Mediation and Arbitration Law,* Article 10.

[36] Ministry of Human Resources and Social Security, *Statistical Bulletin of the Development of Human Resources and Social Security Undertaking of 2010, 2011, 2012.*

[37] Bei Wang, *Labor Dispute Mediation: Case Analysis and Suggestions for Reform,* Social Science Study, 2012, No.6, p. 87.

debate when the *Labor Dispute Mediation and Arbitration Law* was being drafted in 2007. Critics argued that labor dispute resolution procedure tends to retard resolution because it includes both arbitration and litigation and as such too cumbersome compared with regular civil cases, which requires only litigation by a court. Some of them have advocated for either abolishing the requirement about going through arbitration or for requiring either arbitration or litigation but not both.[38] The controversy regarding "singular arbitration, dual trials" continues today. Some scholars oppose the "arbitration first, litigation second" model and call for abolishing this practice. They argue that there is poor legal justification for making labor arbitration a prerequisite for labor litigation, which greatly increases the burden of litigation on the different parties and the court's difficulty in handling labor disputes, and the practice does not promote proper resolution of labor disputes. According to them the concerned parties' will and autonomy should be fully respected, and an "either-or-but-not-both" mechanism should be adopted.[39]

In sum, the purposes of having a special labor dispute resolution mechanism outside regular civil proceedings are to implement the government's public policy, to maintain an amiable relationship between the employer and employee, to mitigate the imbalance between the two, to promote efficient and cost-effective resolution, and to check the number of cases going to the courts. The current model is basically adequate for these purposes. By requiring cases to go through arbitration first, the "singular arbitration, dual trials" model that prevails now has helped to prevent many of them from ending up in the courts directly. And since arbitration procedures tend to be simpler than litigation proceedings, the model facilitates the timely resolution of disputes. Also, the "tripartite" structure, high level of professionalism and democratic character of many arbitration agencies make them suitable for handling labor disputes. Furthermore, this model preserves the court's oversight of arbitration and the different parties' right to sue, which is consistent with the principle of allowing judicial decisions to have finality. For these reasons, the "arbitration first, litigation second" system is quite sensible. This model can give the role of mediation and arbitration full play and can help resolve disputes at the initial stage in a relatively amiable atmosphere as much as possible, possibly avoiding litigation.[40] The model has been in wide use for more than 20 years and has a solid track record.

In conclusion, China should continue the "singular arbitration, dual trials" system. But the process could be improved through reforms measure to streamline litigation proceedings. Appeals about arbitration awards can be filed with the court, but

---

[38] Zengyi Xie, *The Concept, System, and Challenges of Labor Dispute Resolution in China*, CASS *Journal of Law*, 2008, No.5, p. 104.

[39] Guorong Qin, *Choice of Legal Mechanism of Labor Dispute Resolution – Legal Criticism of Labor Arbitration as a Prerequisite Procedure,* Jianghai Journal, 2010, No.3, p. 142.

[40] Chunying Xin (ed.), *Interpretation of the Law on Labor Dispute Arbitration of the People's Republic of China,* Law Press, 2008, pp. 16–17.

only on grounds of matters of law, not of facts. And only cases involving serious and major legal issues can be appealed to the higher court. This mechanism can protect the parties' right to sue, avoid lengthy procedures, and resolve disputes in a timely manner. As for collective labor disputes, especially those involving dispute over "interests" rather than "rights", it is better to resolve them through mediation and arbitration without intervention by the court.

References

Huai Guan, Jia Lin (ed.), *The Labor Law,* Renmin University Press, 2006

Yueqin Huang, *New Commentaries on the Labor Law,* China University of Political Science and Law Press, 2003

Wilhelm Dutz, *Labor Law*, Guowen Zhang trans. Law Press, 2005

Shangyuan Zheng, *The System and Concepts of the Labor Contract Law,* China University of Political Science and Law Press, 2008

Chunying Xin (ed.), *Interpretation of the Labor Contract Law of the People's Republic of China,* Law Press, 2007

Aiqing Zheng, *General Introduction on French Labor Contract Law,* Guangming Daily Press, 2010

Zejian Wang, *Civil Law Theory and Case Study (Vol. 3),* China University of Political Science and Law Press, 1998

Chunying Xin (ed.), *Interpretation of the Law on Labor Dispute Mediation and Arbitration of the People's Republic of China,* Law Press, 2008

Fang Cai (ed.), *China Population and Labor Issues Report, No.10*, Social Sciences Academic Press, 2009

Ming Fan, et al., *Acts of Retirement and Policies of Retirement,* Social Sciences Academic Press, 2008

Jianding Ding & Fengjuan Yang, *The Development of the Social Security System of the United Kingdom,* China Labor and Social Security Press, 2004

Dingjian Cai, *Employment Discrimination in China: Current Conditions and Anti-discrimination Strategies*, China Social Science Press, 2007

Xiaonan Liu (ed.), *Theory and Practice of Antidiscrimination in the Workplace*, Law Press, 2012

Zengyi Xie, *Beyond Employment and Labor Contract Rules – Legislative Concepts and System Building of Protection for Domestic Workers,* Tsinghua Law Review, 2012, No. 6

Xiong Li, *Four Points of Determining the Validity of a Non-Competition Agreement,* Law Application, 2013, No.1

Wei Zhang, *Analysis of Social and Legal Protection for Domestic Workers from the Perspective of Gender Mainstreaming,* Hebei Law Review, 2010, No.8

Minghui Liu, *Obstacles and Approaches for Domestic Workers to Gain the Right to Labor and Social Security Protection*, Journal of the Southwest Nationality University (Liberal Arts and Social Science), 2011, No. 5

Z. Xie, *Labor Law in China*, Research Series on the Chinese Dream and China's Development Path, DOI 10.1007/978-3-662-46929-3

Fang Cai, *The Dilemma of Wage Raise: To Interfere or to Correct the Market?* In Fang Cai (ed.), China Population and Labor Report, No. 14: From Demographic Dividend to Institutional Dividend, Social Sciences Academic Press, 2013

Wenzhen Wang, Kun Huang, *The Tasks and Countermeasures in the Labor Standards Legislation*, China Labor, 2012, No.5

Xinmin Zhang, *Suggestions for Improving the Special Work Hours system in China*, China Labor, 2012, No. 9

The All-China Federation of Trade Unions (ACFTU) Survey Group: *The Survey of China's Current Labor Dispatch Situation,* China Labor, 2012, No. 5

Zengyi Xie, *Labor Dispatch Laws and Regulations of the United States and Ideas for China's Labor Dispatch Legislation*, Comparative Law Study, 2007, No. 6

Ying Jiang, Xin Yang, *On Rights Protection of the Workers in Labor Dispatch – Based on Evidence Analysis of Labor Contract Law Questionnaires*, Academic Journal of National School of Administration, 2011, No.2

Jinfeng Shi, *Study of Labor Dispatch Situation and Countermeasures*, People's Justice, 2009, No. 19

Meiyan Wang, *Implementation of Labor Contract Law: Problems and Countermeasure Suggestions,* Academic Journal of Guizhou College of Finance and Economics, 2013, No.1

Yongqian Tu, *Causes of Labor Dispatch Abuse and Legal Restrictions*, Forum of Political Science and Law, 2013, No.1, p.179

Yanjun Feng, *Doubts and Reflections on the Principle of Equal Pay for Equal Work*, Studies of Law and Commerce, 2011, No. 2

Feifei Ke, Yanlong Jiang, Tiancheng Jiang, *Analysis on Decision Dilemma of Dispatch Workers' Claim of "Equal Pay for Equal Work",* China Labor, 2011, No.12

Rongfang Zhang, *On the Model of China's Legal Restrictions of Labor Dispatch*, Law Review, 2009, No.6

Heping Cai, *The Employee Transfer Law in Germany and Its Development,* in Changzheng Zhou (ed.), The Development of Labor Dispatch and Legal Regulation, China Labor and Social Security Press, 2007

Baohua Dong, *Legal Reflection on Labor Dispatch,* China Labor, 2005, No.6

Jia Lin, Wei Fan, *Analysis of China's Legal Restrictions on Labor Dispatch,* Academic Journal of Renmin University of China, 2011, No. 6

Jia Lin, Fei Yang, *Study of Labor Contract Termination Issues Regarding Severance Allowance, Damages for Breach of Contract, and Damages for Unfair Dismissal,* in Labor Law Review, Jia Lin (ed.), Renmin University Press, 2005

Zengyi Xie, *Study of the Administrative Agency Ordering the Employer to Bear Civil Liabilities,* Contemporary Law Review, 2010, No.3

Labor and Social Security, edited by Beijing Labor and Social Security Law Society, 2013, No.3

Yujuan Zhai, *The Plight and Challenges of Labor Inspection in China – Examples of the Labor Administrative Agency Losing the Case Frequently,* Administration and Law, 2008, No. 5

National Administration of Industry and Commerce: *Nationwide Major Market Development Report*, 3rd Quarter, 2013

Hui Sun, *How Does Labor Inspection Handle Employment Discrimination Cases,* China Labor, 2010, No.11

Ling Tan, *Current Plight and Future Transition of One Arbitration as the Final Ruling for Labor Dispute Cases,* People's Justice, 2012, No.1

Bei Wang, *Labor Dispute Mediation: Case Analysis and Suggestions for Reform,* Social Science Study, 2012, No.6

Zengyi Xie, *The Concept, System, and Challenges of Labor Dispute Resolution in China,* CASS Journal of Law, 2008, No.5

Guorong Qin, *Choice of Legal Mechanism of Labor Dispute Resolution – Legal Criticism of Labor Arbitration as a Prerequisite Procedure,* Jianghai Journal, 2010, No.3

A. C. L. Davies, *Perspectives on Labor Law*, Cambridge University Press, 2004

Manfred Weiss and Marlene Schmidt, Labor Law and Industrial Relations in Germany, Kluwer Law International, 2008

Deborah J Lockton, *Employment Law*, 5th Edition, Palgrave Macmillan, 2006

Blanpain, Bison-Rapp, Corbett, Josephs, and Zimmer, *The Global Workplace: International and Comparative Employment Law-Cases and Materials*, Cambridge University Press, 2007

Stefan Lingemann, Robert von Steinau-Steinruck and Anja Mengel, *Employment and Labor Law in Germany*, Verlag C.H. Beck, 2003

Takashi Araki, *Labor and Employment Law in Japan*, the Japan Institute of Labor, 2002

Mark A. Rothstein, Charles B. Craver, Elinor P. Schroeder, Elaine W. Shoben, *Employment Law*, West, 2005

Simon Deakin & Gillian S Morris, *Labor Law* (Fourth Edition), Hart Publishing, Oxford and Portland, Oregon, 2005

Steven Willborn, Stewart Schwab, John Burton, Gillian Lester, *Employment Law: Cases and Materials*, LexisNexis, 2007

Benjamin W. Wolkinson and Richard N. Block, *Employment Law: The Workplace Rights of Employees and Employers*, Blackwell, 1996

Huge Collins, K.D. Ewing and Aileen McColgan, *Labor law: Text and Materials*, Hart Publishing, Oxford and Portland, Oregon, 2005

Ulla Liukkunen and Chen Yifeng (eds.), "China and ILO Fundamental Principles and Rights at Work" (Bulletin of Comparative Labour Relations), Kluwer Law International, 2014

Gray L. Wickert, *Workers' Compensation Subrogation*, Fourth Edition, Juris Publishing, Inc. 2009

Crystal Roberts, *Far from a Harmonious Society: Employment Discrimination in China*, 52 Santa Clara Law Review, 2012

Timothy Webster, *Ambivalence and Activism: Employment Discrimination in China*, Vanderbilt Journal of Transnational Law, May 2011

Jiefeng Lu, *Employment Discrimination in China: the Current Situation and Principle Challenges*, Hamline Law Review, Winter, 2009

Ronald C. Brown, *China's Employment Discrimination Law During Economic Transition*, 19 Colum. J. Asian L. 361, 2006

Index

Z. Xie, *Labor Law in China*, Research Series on the Chinese Dream and China's Development Path, DOI 10.1007/978-3-662-46929-3

MIX
Papier aus verantwortungsvollen Quellen
Paper from responsible sources
FSC® C105338

If you have any concerns about our products,
you can contact us on
ProductSafety@springernature.com

In case Publisher is established outside the EU,
the EU authorized representative is:
Springer Nature Customer Service Center GmbH
Europaplatz 3, 69115 Heidelberg, Germany

Printed by Libri Plureos GmbH
in Hamburg, Germany